YORK NOTES

General Editors: Professor A.N. Jeffares (*University of Stirling*) & Professor Suheil Bushrui (*American University of Beirut*)

Jane Austen

EMMA

Notes by Barbara Hayley

MA (DUBLIN) PH D (KENT)
Senior Lecturer in English, St Patrick's College, Maynooth

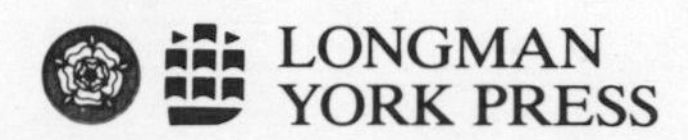

YORK PRESS
Immeuble Esseily, Place Riad Solh, Beirut.

LONGMAN GROUP UK LIMITED
Longman House, Burnt Mill, Harlow,
Essex CM20 2JE, England
and Associated Companies throughout the world.

First published 1981
Reprinted 1988 (twice)

ISBN 0-582-02263-0

Produced by Longman Group (FE) Ltd
Printed in Hong Kong

Contents

Part 1: Introduction	*page* 5
Life of Jane Austen (1775–1817)	5
Historical background	6
Literary background	8
Jane Austen's novels	9
A note on the text	11
Part 2: Summaries	12
A general summary	12
Detailed summaries	16
Part 3: Commentary	50
Subject and scope	51
Structure	59
Plot	62
Characterisation	63
The characters	67
Style	73
Part 4: Hints for study	82
Rereading	82
Chapters for intensive study	84
Characters	86
Style	86
Some sample questions	87
Further questions and model answers	88
Part 5: Suggestions for further reading	91
The author of these notes	93

Part 1

Introduction

Life of Jane Austen (1775–1817)

Jane Austen was born in December 1775, seventh of the eight children of George Austen, a Church of England clergyman, and his wife Cassandra, the daughter of another clergyman; both families had many Church and university connections. The Austens, a happy, well-educated and affectionate family, lived at the rectory in the parish of Steventon in Hampshire from 1764 to 1801 when George Austen retired. Two of Jane Austen's brothers, of whom one had previously been a banker, became clergymen; another inherited land in Kent and Hampshire. Two had distinguished careers in the British Navy, one becoming Commander of the Fleet, the other Commander-in-Chief of the East India Station. As was usual at the time, the daughters did not have careers, but stayed at home, except for visits to friends. Jane and her sister Cassandra went to small boarding schools when very young, but after the age of eleven were educated at home. They read widely in eighteenth-century fiction, played the piano and learnt Italian and French. Jane and Cassandra were devoted to each other throughout Jane's life, and much of our information about her life and opinions comes from her letters written to Cassandra whenever either was away. Jane Austen went to stay for long periods with friends in the counties of Hampshire, Kent, Gloucestershire, Berkshire and Surrey, and also in London. At home, the Austens were popular in their neighbourhood, and accepted by some aristocratic families and 'landed gentry'; they attended many balls, parties and entertainments.

Jane Austen began to write stories and sketches for her family at the age of twelve. By 1795 she had written a comic *History of the World*; an unfinished novel, *Catharine*; and two epistolary novels, *Lady Susan* and *Elinor and Marianne*, which she was later to rewrite as *Sense and Sensibility*. In 1797 she started *First Impressions*, the first draft of *Pride and Prejudice*, and in 1798 *Susan*, which was published after her death as *Northanger Abbey*.

In 1801 the Austen family moved to Bath, a fashionable resort in the south-west of England, famous for its healing spa waters. Jane Austen is reputed to have had a romance in 1802; she parted from her lover, who died in 1803. She had a proposal in 1803 from a wealthy Hampshire landowner; she accepted, but retracted her acceptance the following morning. She never married, but had a full social life with many friends and a large family circle, having numerous nieces and nephews to whom she was very close—in particular her niece Anna, an aspiring novelist with whom she corresponded. After a break in writing from 1801 to 1804, she began *The Watsons*, a novel which she never finished, probably because of the death of her father in 1805.

In 1806 Jane Austen, her sister Cassandra, and their mother moved to Southampton, a large sea-port on the Hampshire coastline, and in 1809 to the village of Chawton, also in Hampshire. It was at Chawton Cottage that she did most of her finished writing. In November 1811 her first published novel, *Sense and Sensibility*, appeared, and was very successful. *Pride and Prejudice* was published in January 1813, *Mansfield Park* in May 1814 and *Emma* in very early 1816. She finished *Persuasion* in July 1816, and began *Sanditon* in 1817, but after two months became too ill to finish it. Her health continued to decline until July of that year when she died, aged only forty-two, and after only five years as a publishing writer. *Northanger Abbey* and *Persuasion* were published in 1818. So the six great novels for which she is remembered all appeared within seven years. They were all published anonymously, and written in secret, though it became know that she was the author, and she was officially requested, against her own wishes, to dedicate *Emma* to the Prince Regent.

Historical background

The period of Jane Austen's life (1775–1817) was one of great disruption in world affairs. The French Revolution of 1789 was the starting-point for similar revolutionary movements in many other countries; and although Great Britain did not have a comparable revolution, she was actively engaged in wars and insurrections all over the world. In 1793 France declared war on her, and from then until just before Jane Austen's death, the two countries were almost continually at war under their great commanders, Napoleon and Wellington. Napoleon was crowned Emperor of France in 1804, and defeated the Austrians in 1805; also in 1805 Admiral Nelson defeated the French fleet at Trafalgar. From 1808 to 1814, Britain was also fighting the Peninsular war against the French in Spain and Portugal. The wars against Napoleon culminated in the battle of Waterloo in 1815 when Wellington and the British, with the help of Blücher and the Prussians, defeated the French under Napoleon; Louis XVIII was restored to the throne of France, and Napoleon was exiled to St Helena.

The Napoleonic wars were not the only military concerns of the British: in 1798 the Irish Rebellion had to be put down; two years later the Act of Union between Great Britain and Ireland was passed, making

Ireland part of Great Britain. From 1799 onwards, Britain was also fighting the Mahratta wars in India. The American War of Independence had come to an end in 1784, with Britain's loss of America as a colony: the newly independent country declared war on Britain in 1812, the war continuing until 1814. Britain had many lesser engagements elsewhere: in 1807 Wellington wrote to the Prime Minister that he was 'ready to set out for any part of the world at a moment's notice', and indeed in that year alone, British forces had engagements in Brazil, Egypt, Sweden and Venezuela.

At home, George III had been king since 1760; in 1810 he became ill and insane and the Regency Bill of 1811 declared his son (later George IV) ruler in his place. As Prince Regent he was politically untrustworthy, as a man he was gross and licentious, but he was remarkable as a leader in fashion and taste. He was pre-eminent in establishing the very distinctive style of his age in architecture, landscape, dress and pastimes. Architecture, after the regular classicism of the preceding age, became ornate and fanciful ('Regency Gothic'), or elaborately 'rustic', or oriental, like the Brighton Pavilion, built for the Prince Regent, with its domes, minarets and Chinese furniture and decorations. With his friend 'Beau' Brummell he set an extremely elegant style of dress for men; not multicoloured and dandyish, but dark and severe; women wore neo-Classical clothes, typically a white muslin dress, simple and flowing, with a high feather headress or turban for grand occasions, or the more usual bonnet for every day. The Prince Regent popularised the idea of staying at seaside resorts such as Weymouth and Brighton, or at fashionable spas such as Bath, all of which appear in Jane Austen's novels. Other places of entertainment with which Jane Austen was familiar through her visits to London included the many theatres; Ranelagh Gardens and Vauxhall Gardens, pleasure gardens for strolling, recreation and refreshment; Almack's Club, the summit of London 'Society', for dancing; Astley's Royal Amphitheatre, for equestrian performances (mentioned in *Emma*, Chapter 54); and a host of other diversions such as music and firework displays on the River Thames.

Jane Austen's letters are full of details about such 'background' on the international and the national level. Her naval brothers were actively engaged in the Napoleonic wars, she had friends and relatives concerned in the Indian uprisings, in the war with America, in the West Indies, even killed in the French Revolution, and all of these places and matters are mentioned in her letters. So are the clothes that she and other people wore. But her novels are not intended to be histories or fashion plates; in them one becomes aware of 'background' only according to the characters' awareness of it. She will not, for example, give a top-to-toe description of a woman's dress, but from Mrs Elton's own words we gather that she has a taste for white and silver poplin, pearls and trimmings (*Emma*, Chapter 35). Because Emma herself is suddenly vividly conscious of the landscape of Mr Knightley's estate, we receive a remarkably clear impression of it (*Emma*, Chapter 42). But unless it was necessary for such purposes, Jane Austen, writing for her contemporaries, avoided self-conscious background and 'current affairs'. She has been criticised for writing at the time of the Napoleonic wars without mentioning them—except in so far as military preparations bring a regiment of militia to Meryton to provide dancing partners for the Bennet sisters in *Pride and Prejudice*. She was, however, intensively and exclusively concerned with the regiment's effect upon the social life of Meryton and the Bennets, and not at all with its effect upon the (unspecified) enemy. She was not eager to load her novels with topical references to events which, however historically important, did not impinge very much on daily life in provincial England, her special domain.

Literary background

Chronologically, Jane Austen's work stands between the neo-Classical formality of the eighteenth century and the effusive, emotional Romanticism of the nineteenth century. It stands at the point where the 'Age of Reason' becomes the 'Age of Sensibility'. But she belongs to no 'school' of writers, and indeed the more her manner, style, or content resembles that of currently popular novelists, the more likely she is to be mocking them. The progress of the novel in England at the end of the eighteenth century did not correspond very closely to the pattern of other kinds of literature, and Jane Austen's style is very much more in tune with that of the poets and non-fictional prose writers of the mid-eighteenth century, the Augustan age. Although Jane Austen read the work of contemporary Romantic poets such as Robert Burns (1759–96), Sir Walter Scott (1771–1832) and Lord Byron (1788–1824), her style and content have much more in common with those of earlier poets such as Alexander Pope (1688–1744), or of essayists and critics such as Joseph Addison (1672–1719) or Samuel Johnson (1709–84). Their extreme formality of style, their balanced sentences, the carefully constructed sequence of their theses are still visible in her prose; their advocation of moderation in all things, their morality, their satirical detachment are echoed in her manner.

The English novel, at the time that Jane Austen was writing, was still in the exciting grip of the Gothic. The Gothic romance was introduced to English literature by Horace Walpole (1717–97) with *The Castle of Otranto* (1765); it rejoiced, or rather agonised, in picturesque horror, magic, superstition, murder and love, against a backdrop of sinister forests and gloomy medieval castles. There are some variations in background, all suitably exotic (William Beckford's *Vathek* (1786) was set in the mysterious east, Mrs Radcliffe's *The Mysteries of Udolpho* (1794) in sixteenth-century France and Italy); and abbeys and monasteries abounded (Mrs Radcliffe's *The Italian* (1797), Matthew Gregory Lewis's *The Monk* (1795)). These and many others brought the supernatural, diabolism, terror and romance to the library tables of the fashionable.

Another vein of novel-writing was pursued by contemporary women writers, notably Fanny Burney (1752–1840) and Maria Edgeworth (1767–1849). Both wrote novels of 'manners'. Fanny Burney's *Evelina* (1778), written in letter form, shows the introduction of a young girl into London society; Maria Edgeworth's *Helen* and *Belinda* also show leisured society (at a more aristocratic level than that in Jane Austen's novels), but are neither as original nor as good as her *Castle Rackrent* (1800) which describes Irish life over several generations, recounted by a peasant, Thady Quirk, in his own dialect. This third vein, the regional one, was to continue well into the nineteenth century. Sir Walter Scott (1771–1832), who had published Scottish ballads *Minstrelsy of the Scottish Border* (1802–3), wrote his first novel, *Waverley*, in 1814, and for the rest of Jane Austen's lifetime continued to write romantic and highly coloured fiction with a Scottish historical setting.

There are echoes of these three kinds of novel in Jane Austen's work. She makes fun of the Gothic novel and its conventions (especially in *Northanger Abbey*, a parody of the genre). Her close examination of social life has much in common with the novel of manners. And she could be said to be preserving in precise detail the manners and customs of provincial England, as other writers were preserving those of Scotland, Wales and Ireland. But June Austen differs from all her contemporaries in the subtlety of her characterisation, in the depth of her irony, and in the individual tone of her narration.

Jane Austen's novels

Jane Austen wrote to her niece Anna, who wished to become a novelist: 'three or four families in a country village is the very thing to work on'; she also described 'the little bit (two inches wide) of ivory on which I work with so fine a brush, as produces little effect after much labour'. The scale of three or four families is that of all Jane Austen's novels; the little bit of ivory is a good image for her intricately detailed work; but her admirers would say that she had laboured to great, not little, effect.

Jane Austen set her 'three or four families' in a rigid hierarchy within their country villages. At a time when the dividing lines between the aristocracy and the upper-middle class, and between the upper-middle class and people in business or 'trade', were becoming blurred, she chose the middle class both as a small, encompassable social span, and as a varied one. Within it she showed a self-defined traditional order of birth, money and land which could only be upset at one's peril. She preaches the conventional pattern of life in the family and in society; the pattern of behaviour expected of one towards family, friends, acquaintances, admirers, superiors and inferiors. The lessons of her novels concern not morals, ethics or religion, but behaviour. One must learn how to behave towards other people; the individual must learn how to fit into society. One of the ways of seeing how to behave is to see clearly: in *Sense and Sensibility*, Marianne Dashwood must abandon her sensibility, or undue emotional sensitivity, before she can behave properly; in *Pride and Prejudice*, Mr Darcy and Elizabeth Bennet must rid themselves, the one of his pride, the other of her prejudice, before they can behave appropriately towards each other and towards others. In *Emma*, the heroine must control her 'fancy', or fantasising imagination, before she can fit herself into what is really happening instead of trying to mould people around her imaginings.

People can be blinded to real life by the preconceptions they have acquired from popular literature; and one of the ways in which Jane Austen represents the realities of life is by pointing out how different it is from what romantic literature would have us believe. From her earliest stories Jane Austen poked fun at the novel of sensibility. *Love and Freindship*, which she wrote at fourteen, is a parody of the sensational romantic novel; much later she wrote a fake synopsis of a novel bringing in all the romantic subjects and backgrounds that her reading and her acquaintances had suggested to her ('Plan of a Novel according to hints from various quarters', about 1816). Marianne Dashwood's sensibility, Emma's fancy, Elizabeth Bennet's prejudice, are ultimately derived from literature. But Jane Austen's funniest and most scathing attack on contemporary literature is in *Northanger Abbey*, in which she turns the Gothic convention on its romantic head. Catherine Morland expects Northanger to be a 'real' Gothic abbey, and is taken aback to find that it is bright and modern instead of mouldering and grim. Her 'passion for ancient edifices' and her 'visions of romance' make her either blind to real life or disappointed in it. In the end, true love triumphs in a rather down-to-earth way and she marries Henry Tilney. Real life is found to be quite different from the expectations of the avid novel-reader. All of Jane Austen's novels end with the typical conclusion of the romantic novel, marriage for two or more of the main characters: the heroine of *Persuasion*, Anne Elliott, has been persuaded eight years ago to renounce her lover, Frederick Wentworth, who reappears on the scene at the beginning of the novel; she is reunited with him at the end of it. But Jane Austen's way of arriving at such last-chapter marriages is not romantic; it is achieved by sweeping away hypocrisy, literary notions, romantic illusions, snobbery and prejudice of all kinds, to arrive at truth, sincerity and a happy union, not just with one's beloved, but with the society in which one finds oneself.

A note on the text

Emma was begun on 21 January 1814 and finished on 29 March 1815. It was published in three volumes in 1816 by John Murray, London. Two thousand copies were printed, of which 1,250 were sold within the year. The second edition appeared in 1833, and the novel was frequently reprinted during the nineteenth century, with an illustrated edition in 1896. One great edition of *Emma* is in the Oxford University Press series of the novels of Jane Austen, edited, with notes and appendices, by R. W. Chapman, Oxford University Press, Oxford, 1923; reprinted twelve times up to 1978. *Emma* also appeared in the Oxford English Novels Series, edited by David Lodge, Oxford University Press, Oxford, 1971. Although the last two are both one-volume editions, they keep to the three-volume scheme, with chapter numbers and pagination corresponding to those of the original three volumes.

The text used in these notes is that of the Penguin edition, edited by Ronald Blythe, Penguin Books, Harmondsworth, 1966; reprinted thirteen times up to 1978. Here the chapter numbers are sequential, in one volume. The Penguin edition's Chapters 1–18 correspond to Volume I, Chapters I-XVIII, of the three-volume edition; Penguin Chapters 19–36 to Volume II, Chapters I-XVIII; Penguin Chapters 37–55 to Volume III, Chapters I-XIX.

Part 2

Summaries
of EMMA

A general summary

Emma has two interconnecting plots. The 'outward' plot is concerned with the comings and goings, advances and reverses of a small circle of moderately well-born people in a provincial town, Highbury. The 'inward' plot is concerned with the mind of the novel's heroine, Emma Woodhouse. The outward plot tells the love stories of three couples, whose weddings are the culmination of the novel: Emma herself and Mr Knightley; Frank Churchill and Jane Fairfax; Harriet Smith and Robert Martin. The inward plot traces the development of Emma's mind from ill-founded self-satisfaction, through several humiliations, to self-knowledge and good sense. The two plots are very closely linked, partly because almost all the 'action' takes place around Emma, but principally because much of it is initiated by her. Her manipulation of the characters around her affects their stories, and also demonstrates her state of mind: her 'fancy', or imaginary perception of what a situation is or might be, leads her and them into many false positions.

The characters whom we first meet around Emma are her indulgent but demanding father; her former governess Mrs Weston and her new husband; and Mr George Knightley, a neighbouring landowner. We later meet her sister Isabella and her husband John, who is Mr Knightley's brother, and other neighbours, including Mrs and Miss Bates and Mr and Mrs Cole. Emma determines to find a wife for Mr Elton, the vicar. When she meets Harriet Smith, who is pretty but not very intelligent, and socially inferior to herself, she decides to befriend her, to 'bring her on', and to marry her to Mr Elton.

Despite Mr Knightley's warnings, Emma brings them together a great deal at her house, Hartfield. She makes Harriet refuse the proposal of marriage she receives from Robert Martin, a tenant farmer on Mr Knightley's estate, whom she does not think grand enough for her protégée. Mr Knightley, who thinks the two ideally matched in rank and education, angrily criticises Emma for interfering, and tells her that Mr Elton will never marry Harriet, who has neither wealth nor rank. They quarrel.

Emma believes her scheme is successful. Mr Elton's constant visits to them, his interest in a portrait she paints of Harriet, the charade or puzzle-poem that he brings them, all make her think that he admires

Harriet—though he does not propose marriage when Emma contrives to leave them alone together. Emma and Mr Knightley make up their quarrel, but she still justifies herself for turning Harriet away from Robert Martin. At a party given by the Westons at their house, Randalls, Mr John Knightley warns Emma that Mr Elton is interested in her, and that her manner towards him is too encouraging. She says he is quite mistaken: her own opinion of Mr Elton is that he is ridiculous and pretentious.

Snow cuts the party short, and Emma find herself returning in a carriage alone with Mr Elton who surprises and distresses her by declaring that he loves her, and cares nothing for Harriet. When she repeatedly repulses him he accuses her of having led him on; both are furious. This scene induces Emma's first period of humiliation: her first inkling that she may have been wrong, that she has misread all the signs, that she has misled Harriet. She despises Mr Elton for his proposal, which she puts down to her wealth and position, but acknowledges that she has appeared too encouraging. She resolves never to matchmake again, and feels great shame for having raised Harriet's expectations, though she still feels that she was right to make her refuse Robert Martin's proposal. Mr Elton goes to Bath. Emma has to tell Harriet what has happened and destroy the hopes that she has built up, though she cannot destroy Harriet's admiration for Mr Elton.

Jane Fairfax, an orphaned granddaughter of Mrs Bates, comes to stay with the Bateses. She has been brought up by a Colonel and Mrs Campbell with their own daughter, now Mrs Dixon. Emma admires her elegance and her accomplished piano-playing and singing, but does not seek her friendship as Mr Knightley thinks she should. Emma is repelled by Miss Fairfax's cold, reserved manner and her tedious relations; Mr Knightley sees that the two young women are of equal education and rank, although Emma is rich and Miss Fairfax is poor. Emma begins to speculate about Jane Fairfax's relationship with the Campbell's son-in-law, Mr Dixon.

News comes that Mr Elton is to be married to a well-to-do lady he has met at Bath. Harriet's shock is blunted by her agitation at meeting Robert Martin and his sisters, who invite her to visit them; Emma ensures that the visit is as short as possible by calling for Harriet herself.

Everyone in Highbury has heard a great deal about Mr Weston's son by his first marriage, now called Frank Churchill, who has been brought up by his uncle and aunt, Mr and Mrs Churchill. His letters are admired: a visit has been promised and postponed many times. At last he arrives; Emma finds him pleasant and charming, and as they walk and talk she feels they have established an instant rapport. It has already crossed her mind that they might be a suitable match for each other. He visits all his father's friends, including Jane Fairfax, whom he has met some months before at Weymouth with the Campbells. Emma questions him closely about Mr Dixon.

Her suspicions about Mr Dixon are increased when an unknown admirer sends Jane Fairfax a piano. Mrs Weston, however, suspects that the sender is Mr Knightley, and that he might marry Miss Fairfax, a prospect which displeases Emma. Frank Churchill criticises Jane Fairfax to Emma, who tells him her suspicions about Mr Dixon: the next day she feels that she has done wrong in gossiping to him. Frank Churchill, who often visits the Bateses, not only encourages Emma in her suspicions but hints about them to Miss Fairfax. He suggests that a ball be held in Highbury, and plans are made, but it is postponed when he has to leave because Mrs Churchill is ill. Before he goes Emma thinks he is on the point of proposing marriage to her: she avoids what she thinks is to be the declaration, and reflects afterwards that he is very much in love with her, but that she is not much in love with him. She now conceives the idea that he should marry Harriet.

Mr Elton returns with his bride, who is treated with all the ceremony attendant upon a newly married woman. She is extremely vulgar, boastful and opinionated. Mr Knightley, on Emma's enquiry, makes it clear that he does not intend to marry Jane Fairfax, but he points out that Emma should have become her friend, and not left her at the mercy of the over-familiar Mrs Elton. Because of her poverty, Jane Fairfax will eventually have to become a governess; Mrs Elton is officiously determined to find her a position immediately. Emma's suspicions about Jane Fairfax are heightened when she hears that she has been seen walking in the rain to the post office—Emma concludes that she has been receiving letters from Mr Dixon.

The long-awaited ball takes place. Frank Churchill is extremely attentive to Emma. Mr Elton openly refuses to dance with Harriet Smith, and Mr Knightley saves her from embarrassment by dancing with her. Emma compares Mr Knightley's manner and appearance favourably with those of all the other men present, and they dance and talk spiritedly together.

The next day, Harriet is set upon by gipsies, and is rescued by Frank Churchill. Emma, seeing them thrown together in this way, thinks how splendid it would be if they married. This time, she resolves not to interfere. Harriet burns her mementoes of Mr Elton. She confesses that she admires someone else whom Emma takes to be Frank Churchill; Emma encourages her to think that she can marry somebody who is her social superior.

Mr Knightley comes to the conclusion that there is a 'private understanding' between Jane Fairfax and Frank Churchill, and that the latter is therefore double-dealing by paying attentions to Emma. He warns Emma of this but she ridicules and denies the possibility. While playing a game with letters, Frank Churchill makes words with private meanings for both Jane Fairfax and Emma. Mrs Elton forces Mr Knightley to invite everyone to his house, Donwell, for the strawberry-picking; while there she presses Jane Fairfax to accept a position as governess which she has found for her. Jane leaves early, distressed and agitated; Frank Churchill arrives late, hot and cross.

At a picnic party at Box Hill, Frank Churchill is dull at first, then becomes animated, and flirts and jokes with Emma. Their banter gets more and more high-spirited, until Emma is thoughtlessly rude to Miss Bates. Mr Knightley makes her realise that she has offended against all her social duties. Another interval of humiliated reflection upon her own conduct follows as she thinks of how badly she has behaved, how cruel she has been to Miss Bates. She pays a penitent visit to the Bateses. Jane Fairfax will not see her; she is going to take the position as governess, and is not well. She continues to refuse all invitations and offers of help from Emma, who now pities her wretched future as a governess, and wishes she had been friendly to her. Mr Knightley is softened by the news that Emma has visited the Bateses.

The unexpected death of Mrs Churchill prevents Frank Churchill from visiting Highbury, so Emma cannot further her plans for him and Harriet, which are still very much in her mind. Then, to her amazement, the Westons receive a letter in which he reveals that he has been secretly engaged to Jane Fairfax since they were at Weymouth, before either came to Highbury. Emma is not upset for herself as had been feared by the Westons, who, like everyone else, had thought that she was the object of Frank Churchill's affections. But in another passage of tormented self-reproach, she considers how she has led Harriet into yet another hopeless and ungrounded love. She is even more distressed when she discovers that she and Harriet have been talking at cross-purposes: it is Mr Knightley's love that Harriet thinks Emma has been encouraging her to hope for. Emma's shock at this news, and her pain when Harriet says that Mr Knightley shows signs of returning her love, make Emma realise that she herself loves Mr Knightley—she could not bear him to marry anyone else. She blames herself for raising Harriet above her station. Just when she thinks that she has lost Mr Knightley to Harriet, he arrives unexpectedly from London and sympathetically asks her her feelings about Frank Churchill's engagement to Jane Fairfax. When he finds she is not at all hurt by it, he declares his own love for her. She returns it, and both are elated. Emma dreads the task of telling Harriet and dashing her hopes again. She asks Isabella to invite her to London.

Emma and Jane Fairfax are reconciled. Mr Knightley plans to live at Hartfield to spare Emma's father from being separated from her, or from having to move to Donwell, but Mr Woodhouse is reluctant to accept any change. Mr Knightley announces that Harriet and Robert

Martin have met in London and are to be married. Emma is relieved of her distress, and finds it a suitable match after all. Frank Churchill and Jane Fairfax return. At last Mr Woodhouse is resigned to the idea of Emma's marriage, and all three couples in sequence get married.

Detailed summaries

Chapter 1

Emma Woodhouse is introduced. Nearly twenty-one years of age, she is mistress of her widowed father's house in the village of Highbury, where they are 'first in consequence', rich and respected. Her former governess, Miss Taylor, has just married Mr Weston, and she misses her company, especially as Mr Woodhouse is not a lively companion. He is anxious about his health, dislikes change, and is a gently selfish man. Mr Knightley, a neighbouring landowner, who is an old friend, visits the Woodhouses after the wedding, which Mr Woodhouse selfishly regrets, but Mr Knightley sees as security, a home and a position in society for Mrs Weston. He discounts Emma's claim that she planned the marriage, and laughingly discourages her when she says that she is now going to find a wife for Mr Elton, the clergyman.

NOTES AND GLOSSARY:

which theatened alloy to her many enjoyments: which threatened to spoil her many enjoyments

bride-people: the newly married couple

valetudinarian: a person constantly concerned with his own ailments

Chapter 2

We hear Mr Weston's history: as a young man of a respectable but not very rich family, he became a captain in the army and married a Miss Churchill, against the wishes of her grand and wealthy family. Since her death, their child Frank has been brought up by Mr and Mrs Churchill, his uncle and aunt, whose surname he has taken. After leaving the army, Mr Weston has made enough money in business to live comfortably, has bought a house called Randalls and married Miss Taylor. She is extremely happy; her only regret is that the Woodhouses will miss her, though they live near enough to visit each other often. Mr Woodhouse thinks she must regret leaving them, and is worried about the effects of the wedding cake on everybody's digestion. Frank Churchill, who is very highly thought of in Highbury, was expected at the wedding but did not come, sending instead a very 'handsome' letter.

NOTES AND GLOSSARY:

succeeding early in life to a small independence: when he was young, Mr Weston had inherited enough money to provide an independent income

entered the militia of his county, then embodied: the militia was a branch of the British military service but not part of the regular army; it was drawn or 'marshalled' from local districts when needed

an easy competence: enough money to make it unnecessary for him to work to earn his living

portionless: without a dowry

Chapter 3

Mr Woodhouse dislikes going out but likes his friends to visit him. They include Mrs Bates, a very old lady, and her daughter Miss Bates, who is talkative, plain and poor, but very well liked for her simplicity and cheerfulness. Mrs Goddard, the headmistress of a boarding school, joins them to play cards, and one evening brings an older pupil, Harriet Smith, whom Emma finds pretty, well-mannered, and grateful for her attention. She decides to improve Harriet, and to introduce her to the best society in Highbury. She feels that Harriet's own friends must be inferior and unpolished, in particular a farming family called Martin with whom she has stayed. The splendid supper which concludes the evening is as usual a trial for Mr Woodhouse, torn between the desire to provide hospitably for his friends and to spare their digestions from rich food. He himself eats gruel, a liquid food for invalids.

NOTES AND GLOSSARY:

to make up a card-table for him: to invite enough people for a game of cards

quadrille: a card game for four people using forty cards

fancy-work: pieces of ornamental needlework

parlour-boarder: a boarding-school pupil who lives with the family of the principal

Chapter 4

Harriet Smith becomes Emma's friend and companion. Emma unsuccessfully tries to find out who this illegitimate girl's parents are. She discourages Harriet's friendship with the Martins, particularly the unmarried son Robert, who, she tells Harriet, is too low in rank, too young, and too poor to marry. She encourages Harriet to believe that she can rise in society. Out walking, they meet Mr Martin, and after

Harriet has spoken to him, Emma bluntly tells her that he is plain, ungraceful and ungentlemanly, unlike her own friends—especially Mr Elton, upon whom she has fixed to marry Harriet.

NOTES AND GLOSSARY:

Elegant Extracts: a periodical anthology of excerpts from other books. The verse that Mr Woodhouse admires in Chapter 9 is copied from it

The Vicar of Wakefield: a gently comic novel (1766) by Oliver Goldsmith (1730–94). Harriet fears that Mr Martin is not fashionable in his reading, which is either practical *(The Agricultural Reports)*, superficial or out of date

The Romance of the Forest: a Gothic tale (1791) interspersed with pieces of poetry, by Mrs Ann Radcliffe (1764–1823)

Children of the Abbey: A Tale: another romantic horror novel (1798), by Regina Maria Roche (1764–1845)

to be ... beforehand with the world: to have money in hand for future contingencies

money ... all afloat, all employed in his stock: his money is all in use, put into his farm animals. Notice the importance of money in the novel—Mr Weston's wealth is assessed (Chapter 2); Mr Knightley comments on the security Mrs Weston has now she is married (Chapter 1) and says that Mr Elton will marry for money (Chapter 8), which he does (Chapter 22)

want of gentility: lack of gentlemanly qualities

without air: unstylish

genteel: polished, well-bred. 'Gentility' is of great importance in Highbury society: one must look and behave like a gentleman or lady, even if one is not highly born

Chapter 5

Mr Knightley and Mrs Weston discuss Emma's friendship with Harriet, of which he disapproves. He considers that Harriet's inferiority in rank and lack of education make her an unsuitable companion for Emma, and that Harriet will grow used to grander people than her own natural friends. He also considers that Emma suffers from a vanity more subtle than personal vanity. Mrs Weston does not consider the friendship harmful, and thinks that Emma will make few errors, none of them lasting. Both agree that Emma is very pleasing in appearance. They inconclusively discuss the prospects of her marrying: he feels she needs to fall in love, preferably with someone of whose love for her she is not certain.

NOTES AND GLOSSARY:

a subjection of the fancy to the understanding: Mr Knightley thinks that Emma will never do anything that requires her intellect to overcome her imagination. Emma's 'fancy' is one of the novel's principal concerns: it leads to all her mistakes and misunderstandings

from the wantonness of comfort: from excessive comfort

out of conceit with: dissatisfied with

spleen: ill humour

this little remains of office: this small part left over from her governess's position; she is resuming for a moment her old responsibility for Emma

Chapter 6

Emma thinks her plans for marrying Harriet to Mr Elton are succeeding: Harriet admires him, and he sees the improvements that Emma's influence have made to her manner and character. Emma remarks that they have no picture of Harriet, and Mr Elton persuades her to paint one. They admire her earlier drawings—all unfinished. She starts a full-length watercolour portrait and Mr Elton reads aloud while Harriet poses. The finished picture is warmly praised by Mr Elton, who offers to take it to London to be framed.

NOTES AND GLOSSARY:

Did you ever have your likeness taken?: Did anyone ever paint a portrait of you?

I took him: I drew a picture of him

cockade: here, the plume of hair on his head; usually, a rosette or ribbon on a hat

the declaration: the declaration of love, or proposal of marriage. This is the culmination of any courtship, and in *Emma* many scenes hinge on it: Mr Elton's unwelcome one to Emma, in the carriage (Chapter 15); Mr Knightley's welcome one (Chapter 49). Emma, mistakenly thinking that Frank Churchill is going to make a declaration to her, deflects it (Chapter 30); Robert Martin makes his to Harriet by letter (Chapter 7). The declaration was understood to entail a proposal of marriage

complaisance: desire to please

Chapter 7

Harriet is confused by a letter from Robert Martin proposing marriage. Emma is surprised that the letter is well written, but is convinced that Harriet should refuse him. She agrees somewhat reluctantly and Emma explains that to accept him would have been to end her friendship with Emma, who could never have been the friend of a farmer's wife. Harriet sorrowfully, with help from Emma, writes a letter of refusal. Emma distracts and cheers her by imagining Mr Elton showing her portrait to his family.

NOTES AND GLOSSARY:

the purport of your answer: what your answer should convey
I collect: I gather, I infer

Chapter 8

Mr Knightley talks to Emma about Harriet, praising her beauty and the improvements that Emma has made in her. He is delighted to tell Emma that someone is about to propose to Harriet. She hopes it is Mr Elton, but it is Robert Martin, who has consulted Mr Knightley and been encouraged. He is furious that Harriet has already refused, and accuses Emma of giving her ideas above her station. They quarrel, Emma defending herself and Harriet for the refusal but feeling rather uneasy. She puts forward Mr Elton, who, Mr Knightley says, will never marry a woman without rank or money. Emma is worried that Harriet may have met Robert Martin and weakened; but she returns full of talk about Mr Elton.

NOTES AND GLOSSARY:

settled provision: money legally settled upon or given to her
canvassing it: asking for support for it
restoratives: medicines or drinks that bring back one's strength

Chapter 9

Despite Mr Knightley's disapproval, Emma proceeds with her scheme. Harriet grows increasingly attached to Mr Elton: Emma's plan to educate her by reading literature with her is less successful, and is reduced to the compiling of a collection of riddles, with which they ask Mr Elton to help them. He brings them a charade or puzzle in verse (which he claims was written by a friend) with the solution 'Courtship', which Emma takes to point to an interest in Harriet, whom she congratulates on her prospects of marrying him. Harriet is flattered and excited at the thought. Mr Woodhouse admires the verses. He and Emma make plans for the visit of her sister Isabella, who is married to Mr Knightley's brother John. Emma is amused by Mr Elton's awkward and pompous way of accepting the honour of having the verses of his 'friend' copied into the collection.

NOTES AND GLOSSARY:

a thin quarto of hot-pressed paper: a slim 'book', which they have made by folding best-quality paper

in this age of literature, such collections on a very grand scale: the narrator is being sarcastic; the riddles collected hardly consitute 'literature'

'Kitty, a fair but frozen maid': from a riddle by David Garrick, a well-known actor (1717–79), published in the *New Foundling Hospital for Wit*, Part IV (1771). It links Cupid (the god of love) and a chimney-sweep

enigmas, charades or conundrums: puzzles of various kinds. An enigma is a riddle; a charade is a puzzle in which each syllable of a word must be guessed; a conundrum involves a pun or play on words

the only security of its freshness: the only way of making sure it has not been used before

my first doth affliction denote: woe

which my second is destined to feel: man. The answer to the charade is 'wo[e]man', the best cure for that affliction

The course of true love never did run smooth: a quotation from *A Midsummer Night's Dream* (I.1.134) by William Shakespeare (1564–1616)

all *appropriation*: all that makes the whole verse belong to one particular person (Emma thinks he means Harriet)

having made a push: having made a determined advance (a military phrase)

having thrown a die: having made a decisive step (that is, cast a dice that would decide the course of action)

sure of his rubber: sure of having enough people to play cards

effusion: literary composition that is an outpouring of the author's feelings

---

Chapter 10

Visiting a poor villager, Emma and Harriet pass Mr Elton's house, and Emma thinks of the calls she will make there when Harriet becomes Mrs Elton. Harriet wonders why Emma has not married: Emma replies that she is waiting for 'somebody very superior to any one I have seen yet'.

She has enough 'fortune', 'employment' and 'consequence', that is, money, occupation and importance, and she is the mistress of her father's house and his affection. Her mind is active; she does not dread as Harriet does, the state of being 'an old maid'. Miss Bates, for example, is well liked; she is 'only too good natured and too silly' to suit Emma—whom she particularly bores by chattering about her niece Jane Fairfax. They meet Mr Elton; Emma contrives to leave Harriet alone with him by pretending her bootlace is broken; but he does not 'come to the point', that is, propose.

NOTES AND GLOSSARY:

considering exteriors and probabilities considering what it looked like outside, and what it probably looked like inside. Emma here compares Harriet's enthusiasm for the vicarage with Mr Elton's supposed praise of Harriet's 'ready wit' (he meant Emma's). She finds both ridiculous, and only fit for people in love

the pattern of a stomacher: instructions for making an ornamental bodice

half-boot: a boot reaching to between the ankle and knee

Chapter 11

Emma's sister Isabella and her husband Mr John Knightley come to stay at Hartfield with their five children. They discuss the Westons, Isabella and her father still thinking it sad that Mrs Weston should have left Hartfield whereas Emma and Mr John Knightley think she is very happy. Frank Churchill and his 'handsome letter' are mentioned. Isabella feels his absence from home must be 'shocking' for his father; Mr John Knightley considers it suits Mr Weston quite well, as he likes society as much as his domestic ties.

NOTES AND GLOSSARY:

Mr Knightley; Mr John Knightley: the elder brother's Christian name is George, the younger's John. The elder is addressed and described as 'Mr Knightley', whereas any younger brothers are called by Christian name and surname, as 'Mr John Knightley'. Similarly, the eldest unmarried daughter is called only by her surname, as 'Miss Woodhouse', any younger daughters being addressed by both names. Before Isabella's marriage, she would have been 'Miss Woodhouse' and Emma 'Miss Emma Woodhouse'; now Emma is the 'eldest' (and only) unmarried daughter, so she is 'Miss Woodhouse'

which she wanted: which she lacked
any doubts of the air of Randalls: any doubts as to whether or not the air there is healthy
where is the young man?: he means Frank Churchill
to look down on the common rate of social intercourse: to despise the ordinary course of friendship and visiting outside his own home, which was 'all-sufficient' or enough for him
her brother: frequently used where we would now say 'brother-in-law'

Chapter 12

Mr Knightley and Emma make up their quarrel while playing with their shared niece. Emma does not yield in her conviction that she was right to set Harriet against Mr Martin; Mr Knightley, her elder by sixteen years, considers that she is guided by fancy and whim in her judgements of men and women and in the way she manipulates them. Mr Knightley and his brother converse with undemonstrative brotherly affection; Mr Woodhouse and Isabella discuss health, doctors and diseases, which are sources of great interest to them both, along with the sea air and the healthiest places for holidays. Isabella thinks that Jane Fairfax would be 'a delightful companion for Emma'.

NOTES AND GLOSSARY:
under the power of fancy and whim: her fancy is romantic imagination and whims are capricious ideas. Mr Knightley is pinning down Emma's failings in her dealings with adults: she lets her imagination run away with her, whereas when she is dealing with children, she is guided by 'nature', that is, things as they really are. The central theme of the novel is the disciplining of Emma's 'fancy' (see note on Chapter 5)

Chapter 13

Isabella's stay passes happily, and they visit many friends. Mr Weston insists that the Woodhouse family pay an evening visit to Randalls, and even Mr Woodhouse, who detests dining out in the evening, accepts the invitation. Harriet, Mr Elton and Mr Knightley are also invited. Harriet develops a fever and a sore throat, so has to miss the party; Emma tries to persuade Mr Elton that he should stay away to enquire about Harriet's health, but he seems unconcerned about it, and only worried lest Emma catch the infection. Mr John Knightley suggests that Mr

Elton is in love with Emma herself, which astonishes her; he also suggests that her manner towards Mr Elton is encouraging, which displeases her. Mr John Knightley dislikes the prospect of setting forth, and considers it absurd and conceited of anyone to force them out to visit him.

NOTES AND GLOSSARY:

Mr Elton's objects: the object of his affections, that is, his beloved

that very day se'nnight: that day week (se'nnight being seven nights, as a fortnight is fourteen)

Chapter 14

The Woodhouse party arrives at Randalls, and Emma is annoyed to find Mr Elton seated beside her at dinner, and excessively attentive. She remembers Mr John Knightley's warning that Mr Elton is interested in her, not in Harriet. She is intrigued by a conversation about Frank Churchill because, although she says she will never marry, 'if she *were* to marry he was the very person to suit her in age, character and condition'. She hopes to meet him one day, and Mrs Weston expects that he will be visiting them within a fortnight—though that depends on the arrangements of his aunt, Mrs Churchill, who is difficult and possessive.

NOTES AND GLOSSARY:

to be sitting long after dinner: it was customary for the ladies to withdraw from the dining-room to the drawing-room after dinner, while the gentlemen remained to drink port, joining the ladies later

Chapter 15

When the gentlemen join the ladies after dinner, Mr Elton's concern still seems to be for Emma rather than for Harriet; this public interest in herself offends Emma. Mr John Knightley announces that it is snowing hard, and everyone becomes agitated about the return home. Only Mr Knightley has the calmness to look at the roads; he proclaims them safe. On the drive home, Emma finds herself alone in the second carriage with Mr Elton, and is aghast when he declares his love for her. She mentions Harriet, whom he disregards, saying he has 'never thought of Miss Smith' in his life. All he has said, all his attentions, have been directed to Emma, to mark 'his adoration'. He takes her stunned silence for acceptance of his love. She again mentions Harriet, whom he again discounts, claiming that Emma has 'encouraged' him. She tells him she has 'no thoughts of matrimony at present', speaking so bluntly that he is angry and resentful. They part coldly when the carriage reaches

Hartfield, and the affectionate welcome of her family is contrasted with Emma's deep distress.

NOTES AND GLOSSARY:

order the carriage . . . carriages spoken for: their own carriages, in which they had arrived, were waiting for them in the stables, and they simply had to send word (speak) for them to be brought round

the sweep: the curved carriage-drive leading to a house

her subject cut up: her subject of conversation cut short

his half and half state: she thinks he is half drunk and half sober

Chapter 16

Emma is overwhelmed with misery and humiliation after Mr Elton's declaration. She sees that she has made a mistake, has subordinated everything to her original fantasy, and has done great harm to Harriet. She has misinterpreted all Mr Elton's speeches, and remembers Mr John Knightley's warning that Mr Elton was interested in her herself, and Mr Knightley's that he would never marry Harriet. She despises Mr Elton and feels that he only wanted to marry her to better himself socially and financially, but in honesty she admits to herself that her behaviour to him has indeed seemed encouraging. She sees that 'it was foolish, it was wrong, to take so active a part in bringing any two people together': ashamed, she resolves never to do so again. She still feels, however, that she was right to make Harriet reject Robert Martin, and even finds herself thinking of another more fitting suitor for her. She is resilient enough to recover by the next day but she still has ahead of her the task of explaining to Harriet what has happened.

NOTES AND GLOSSARY:

Emma sat down to think and be miserable: this is the 'relief of quiet reflection' promised at the end of the preceding chapter, and it is the first of several occasions in which Emma, alone and humiliated, reflects on what has happened and shifts her perspective to accommodate her new perceptions. Now she understands what Mr Elton meant by his charade, by his praise of the portrait, by his phrase 'no married people at present'; and in that understanding she realises how her own behaviour has appeared. She also understands that she has done 'evil to Harriet' in meddling with her affections. Similar reflection occurs in Chapters 44 and 47

Chapter 17

Mr and Mrs John Knightley and their children leave. Mr Elton writes to Mr Woodhouse (without mentioning Emma) to say that he is going to Bath for several weeks. Emma confesses to Harriet what has happened, exposing her own misjudgement and destroying Harriet's hopes. Harriet weeps but 'blames nobody', and is humble, modest and simple in her disappointment. Emma resolves to repress her own imagination and so help Harriet. She tries to 'drive Mr Elton from her thoughts', for poor Harriet proves to have been seriously in love with him. Emma insensitively fails to understand how she can be in love with someone who does not love her.

NOTES AND GLOSSARY:

Bath: a famous and fashionable health spa and resort in the south-west of England (Jane Austen lived there for a few years)

she had not even a share in his opening compliments: his letter does not mention Emma at all, even at the beginning, as 'Dear Mr and Miss Woodhouse', or 'May I offer to you and Miss Woodhouse...'

Chapter 18

Frank Churchill does not, after all, come to Highbury, to Mrs Weston's great disappointment. Although Emma does not greatly care at present whether he is there or not, she agrees that his absence is a great loss, and that the Churchills are to blame for preventing him from coming. She even finds herself defending him against Mr Knightley, who thinks that Frank Churchill could have come if he had wanted to, and is neglecting his duty by not visiting his father and new stepmother: any man of sense would have told Mrs Churchill directly that his duty to his father demanded a visit. Emma defends Frank Churchill because he is dependent financially on the Churchills. Mr Knightley despises his much admired letters and foresees that when he does arrive he will be insufferable. Emma thinks they are both prejudiced ('You against, I for him'); she is perplexed by Mr Knightley's vexation.

Chapter 19

Emma and Harriet, having been 'talking enough of Mr Elton that day' (everything reminds Harriet of Mr Elton), go to see Mrs and Miss Bates. Mr Knightley and a few other people think that Emma is not kind enough to these ladies; she considers them tiresome, and not at the highest level of Highbury society. They are warmly welcomed, Miss Bates overpowering them with her fast, repetitive flow of words. The conversation unfortunately turns to Mr Elton, and, even worse for Emma, to Jane Fairfax and a letter which the Bateses have received from her. She is coming soon to stay with them for three months, as the Campbells, with whom she has been living, are going to Ireland to stay with their daughter, Mrs Dixon. From Miss Bates's references to Mr Dixon and Jane Fairfax, Emma gets a suspicion that there is some connection between them, especially when she finds out that Mr Dixon has once saved Jane Fairfax from drowning. Having heard all the news Emma escapes without actually having the letter read to her.

NOTES AND GLOSSARY:

my huswife: a small case containing scissors, thread, needles and other sewing things

she fills the whole paper and crosses half: when she has finished writing a page, she turns it sideways and writes at right angles to what is already written—hence 'chequerwork', the criss-cross effect. This was quite usual up to the end of the nineteenth century

out of rule: not at her usual time

must make it very strange ... countries: after the Act of Union between Great Britain and Ireland in 1801, the two *countries* were part of the same *kingdom*

Chapter 20

Jane Fairfax is introduced: she is the orphaned daughter of an army lieutenant, and as Mrs and Miss Bates are her only relatives, her financial and social prospects are very limited. She has, however, been brought up by Colonel Campbell, whose life her father once saved. He and his wife have educated her as well as their own daughter, now Mrs Dixon, her close friend. Although her circumstances with the Campbells have been comfortable, her future is less inviting: the only opportunity for a fortuneless girl is to become a governess, which she has decided to do when she is twenty-one, though the Campbells wish to keep her with them until she has recovered her health. Now she has arrived in Highbury, to the regret of Emma, who dislikes her for several reasons: everyone wants them to be friends; Jane Fairfax is cold and indifferent; her aunt talks too much. Mr Knightley thinks that Emma dislikes her because she sees in her the accomplished young woman she herself would like to be. Her elegance and beauty and the equality of their education ought to recommend her to Emma. Emma resolves to think more favourably of her, and to pity her for her coming fate as a governess. She muses on the attachment she suspects between Jane Fairfax and Mr Dixon—and even forgives her for it. But Emma's new benevolence is cut short when Jane Fairfax visits Hartfield with the Bateses; she finds Miss Bates tiresome and prolix, and Jane Fairfax condescending, cold, and over-reticent about the Dixons and Frank Churchill, whom she has met at Weymouth.

NOTES AND GLOSSARY:

camp-fever: name given to epidemics occurring in military camps, chiefly typhus

Though his income . . . moderate: the money he earned in the army and his allowances from it were large, but his own private capital was not

noviciate: a novice or probationer in a religious order. Jane sees herself as about to quit the pleasures of society as finally as if she were about to become a nun

cavil: to make frivolous objections

disgustingly: this word was not as strong as we might consider it today; here read 'aggravatingly'

watering-place: a fashionable holiday resort, where one could bathe in the sea, or bathe in or drink the waters of a mineral spring

Weymouth: a seaside resort in the south-west of England

Chapter 21

Mr Knightley is pleased that Emma appears to be more attentive to Jane Fairfax. Miss Bates brings the news that Mr Elton is to be married to a Miss Hawkins whom he has met at Bath. There is much excitement and speculation, interspersed with praise for the hindquarter of pork that the Woodhouses have given the Bateses. Emma is wondering how best to tell Harriet that Mr Elton is to be married when she bursts in full of her own news—she has met Mr Robert Martin and his sister in a shop. They have been kind and pleasant to her; even Emma finds that they have been sensitive and tactful. Emma distracts her from them with the news about Mr Elton, reflecting that as Harriet is so frequently at Hartfield, they will not easily be able to reach her.

NOTES AND GLOSSARY:

muffin: a light, flat, spongy cake, eaten toasted and buttered

spencer: a woman's close-fitting jacket

'our lot is cast in a goodly heritage': Miss Bates is misquoting the Bible (Psalms 16:7), 'The lot is fallen unto me in a fair ground; yea, I have a goodly heritage'

Chapter 22

All Highbury is intensely interested in Mr Elton's bride-to-be. He returns delighted with his choice—she possesses 'so many thousands as would always be called ten'. He has found 'both fortune and affection'. Emma thinks there will be less embarrassment between herself and Mr Elton when he is married; Harriet is still pining for him and cannot be 'talked out of love', especially as everybody is discussing him. But she is equally upset about the Martins; Miss Martin has called on her. How should she return the visit? Emma decides that she will leave Harriet at the Martins' house for a short time and return to collect her, so that the visit will be polite, detached and brief.

NOTES AND GLOSSARY:

a Bristol—merchant, of course, he must be called: the narrator hesitates before describing Miss Hawkins's father as a merchant, because it was considered very ungentlemanly to be 'in trade'. The narrator then goes on to surmise, more unkindly, that as his profits were small, there was not much 'dignity' attached to his 'line of trade', that is, the thing that he sold

drudge: a hack, someone employed in menial work

Chapter 23

Harriet visits Mrs Martin and her two daughters. Just as they are regaining their past friendliness after a reserved beginning, Emma arrives in her carriage to collect Harriet. This brief visit shows how little she esteems them ('Fourteen minutes to be given to those with whom she had thankfully passed six weeks not six months ago!'). Emma realises how hard it is for them all, and wishes that the Martins were of higher rank, so that they would not be 'beneath' Harriet. Tired out with all these considerations, she goes to call on the Westons at Randalls, misses them there and meets them at Hartfield where they are calling on her and her father, with the great news that Frank Churchill is about to arrive at last, the next day. Emma relishes 'the freshness of what was coming'. He arrives early and Mr Weston brings him to Hartfield. His appearance is 'unexceptionable', his face spirited and lively. Emma finds him very charming, and full of praise for Randalls and for his stepmother. Emma fleetingly wonders if he is aware of 'what might be expected from their knowing each other'—that is, that they might marry. Frank Churchill mentions that he intends to call on a young lady he met at Weymouth—Miss Fairfax. His father urges him to do so quickly; he does not respond very enthusiastically when Emma remarks that Miss Fairfax is very elegant. As he leaves with Mr Weston, Emma reflects that it has been a very pleasant start to their acquaintance.

NOTES AND GLOSSARY:

his son, too well bred to hear the hint, rose immediately also: Frank is too polite to hear his father's hint (about having errands to do, but not wishing to disturb anyone else) without taking action upon it

Chapter 24

The next morning, Frank Churchill comes to Hartfield again, with Mrs Weston. He finds Highbury delightful, and Emma rejoices to see how agreeable he is to Mrs Weston; she decides that Mr Knightley was wrong to think him insincere. As they pass the Crown Inn, Churchill remarks upon its large, unused ballroom and thinks they should hold a ball despite the lack of 'proper' or upper-class families; they should ask everyone they know. Emma is doubtful about the mixture of ranks. She enquires about his visit to the Bateses: he has been overwhelmed by the 'talking aunt', Miss Bates, about whom Emma has warned him; he has found Miss Fairfax looking ill and pale. He will not agree with Emma's defence of her complexion and appearance. Emma asks if he has seen Miss Fairfax much but he remarks on Ford's shop which they are just passing; later he replies jokingly and evasively. Emma brings up Jane Fairfax's situation in life, a conversation from which Mrs Weston smilingly withdraws, having been a governess herself. Emma praises Jane Fairfax's piano playing, and he reveals that Mr Dixon, even when engaged to Miss Campbell, now his wife, preferred Miss Fairfax's playing to hers. Emma says she finds Miss Fairfax cold and reserved, which he agrees is an unattractive quality—'one cannot love a reserved person'. Emma is very favourably impressed with him, 'after walking together so long, and thinking so much alike'. She thinks his praise for Mr Elton's small house shows him willing to give up the splendours of the Churchills' house for a smaller establishment of his own.

NOTES AND GLOSSARY:

post-horses: horses ready to be ridden forward to the next 'stage' with mail, and to furnish a change of horses for the person carrying the mail—or for coaches

his indifference to a confusion of rank, bordered too much on inelegance of mind: Emma thinks that Frank Churchill almost lacks refinement because he is willing to mix well-born people with their inferiors

cried up: praised

repulsive: not as strong a word as it is now; here, unattractive

the inroads on domestic peace to be occasioned by no housekeeper's room, or a bad butler's pantry: he might not realise how difficult it is to live harmoniously in a small house that does not have space enough for the servants

Chapter 25

Emma's favourable opinion of Frank Churchill is shaken when he goes to London next day, merely to have his hair cut; but she is pleased to hear that he finds her beautiful and charming, according to Mr Weston. Highbury thinks well of him, apart from Mr Knightley, who is inflexible in his poor opinion of him.

Emma asks the Westons' advice on whether she should go to the Coles' party. They are of low birth, but have become rich through trade; Emma had decided not to accept any invitation from them, but in fact they have invited all her friends and not herself. Finally, an invitation comes for her—should she accept? The Westons press her to do so, and Emma begins to revise her views about the Coles, who are very considerate of her own and her father's comfort. She accepts, and makes arrangements for friends to keep Mr Woodhouse company at home as he hates going out. He is worried lest Emma gets tired at the party.

NOTES AND GLOSSARY:

piquet: a card game for two persons, played with thirty cards of the pack

Chapter 26

Frank Churchill returns from London, having had his hair cut. Emma 'moralises' to herself that 'wickedness is always wickedness, but folly is not always folly'. She looks forward to seeing him at the Coles' party which she means to enjoy despite her scruples about them; she wonders what his manner towards her means, and what people will think when they see them together. Leaving Miss Bates and Mrs Goddard to play cards with her father, she arrives at the party just after Mr Knightley, who, she observes, has come in his carriage in a suitably gentlemanly way. Mrs Cole tells them that somebody has sent Jane Fairfax a piano; nobody knows who, but the general conclusion is that it must be Colonel Campbell. Emma confides to Frank Churchill her suspicions that the gift is from Mr Dixon, who, she thinks, is in love with Jane Fairfax. She uses the fact that Mr Dixon saved Miss Fairfax from drowning to confirm her theory and is surprised to find that Frank Churchill was there when the accident happened. She thinks she has convinced him.

Frank Churchill comes to sit next to Emma, who thinks she is 'his object, and every body must perceive it'. She notices him looking intently at Jane Fairfax and he explains that she has done her hair eccentrically; he goes to speak to her about it. Mrs Weston tells her that Mr Knightley has arranged for his carriage to bring Jane Fairfax and take her home: she also surmises that it is Mr Knightley who sent the piano, and that he may marry Miss Fairfax, a notion that Emma thinks out of the question, though it disturbs her. Emma and Jane Fairfax each play and sing, and Frank Churchill sings with both. Emma discusses Miss Fairfax's piano with Mr Knightley, and is convinced that he did not send it. Frank Churchill dances with Emma, and says that her style of dancing suits him better than Jane Fairfax's languid style would have done.

NOTES AND GLOSSARY:

'Mr Knightley, he is *not* a trifling, silly young man': although Emma is moralising 'to herself', she is mentally speaking to Mr Knightley, contradicting his criticism of Frank Churchill

a large-sized square pianoforte: the forerunner of the modern piano, a rectangular instrument but with its strings parallel to the keyboard, not at right angles. Broadwoods were among the most famous makers

spinet: a small musical instrument like a harpsichord but less grand (and less modern than a pianoforte)

a grand pianoforte: a larger instrument than the square pianoforte, its case harp-shaped, not rectangular

a rather long interval ... exactly right: each 'course' consisted of a great number of different things to eat; the dishes were set out formally down the middle and at the corners of the table. 'Between courses', what was on the table was removed, and replaced with the next group of dishes. A daring and intimate conversation such as Emma was having with Frank Churchill had to wait until the servants had gone, and everyone was talking and eating again

the rest of the dinner ... children came in: after the dinner proper was finished, fruit and sweetmeats were brought in, and it was customary for the children of the family, who did not dine with the adults, to come in at this point to talk to their parents and their guests

its tone, touch and pedal: the quality of its sound, the way in which it responds to the player, and the way in which it became louder as one touched its pedal

you would not have little Henry cut out from Donwell: if Mr Knightley marries and has a son, his estate will go to that son on his death, whereas if he has no heir, his brother John will inherit, and after that, his elder son Henry
put-to: harness horses and attach them to the carriage
was seated: at the piano

Chapter 27

Reflecting on the party the next day, Emma is pleased with her success, but fears that she has been indiscreet in discussing Jane Fairfax's feelings with Frank Churchill. She also regrets that she cannot play or sing as well as Jane Fairfax because she does not practise enough. She starts to do so, but Harriet arrives and praises her playing. The Coxes have talked to Harriet and Robert Martin, who has dined with them. At Ford's shop, Emma and Harriet meet Mrs Weston and Frank, who are going to hear the new piano; Miss Bates asks Emma and Harriet to come too. They go, to a torrent of words about her mother's broken spectacles, Miss Fairfax's lack of appetite, the apples that Mr Knightley has sent them, and the dangers of the stairs.

NOTES AND GLOSSARY:
a mind lively and at ease ... answer: when a mind is lively and easy, everything it sees serves a purpose (that is, keeps it busy)
figured: patterned

Chapter 28

They arrive to find Frank Churchill mending the spectacles, and Jane Fairfax 'intent upon her pianoforte', which she eventually plays for them. Frank Churchill drops hints to Emma about 'Colonel Campbell and his party', referring to her guess about Mr Dixon. Jane Fairfax with 'enforced calmness' avoids discussing the Campbells, and even asks Frank to stop—but Emma thinks that she is feeling guilty pleasure at the gift of the piano. Emma feels half ashamed of her suspicion, but Frank Churchill declares it the key to all Jane Fairfax's behaviour. Mr Knightley passes and Miss Bates talks to him through the window.

NOTES AND GLOSSARY:
her usual employment: that is, reading
deedily: busily
do put up your horse at the Crown: leave your horse at the coaching inn for a while

Chapter 29

Frank Churchill thinks there should be another dance, and starts to plan it with Emma and Mrs Weston. Randalls being too small, the Crown Inn is suggested, inspected and decided on. Miss Bates and Jane Fairfax are brought along as advisers, on Frank Churchill's suggestion.

NOTES AND GLOSSARY:

worth while to stand up: that is, enough couples to make a suitable number for an organised dance

Chapter 30

Frank Churchill receives permission from the Churchills to prolong his stay for the ball. Two days later, however, they request his return as Mrs Churchill is ill. The ball must be abandoned. He comes to pay his farewell to the Woodhouses, having already said goodbye to the Bateses and Jane Fairfax. Emma feels he is on the point of saying something serious to herself but forestalls it. She is sure that he is in love with her, and that she is in love with him. She is disappointed about the ball; Mr Knightley is sorry for her disappointment; Jane Fairfax is composed, but has not been well.

NOTES AND GLOSSARY:

to trifle: to speak in a frivolous way about something serious

I think you can hardly be quite without suspicion: Frank Churchill is about to ask Emma about Jane Fairfax, whom he has just been visiting and talking about. Surely, he feels, Emma must suspect his interest in Jane Fairfax. To Emma, however, his words 'seemed like the forerunner of something absolutely serious' which she thinks is going to be a declaration of love for herself

visit: it was polite practice to call on friends, however briefly, to say goodbye. (In his next letter, Frank Churchill sends his adieux to Harriet, whom he has not managed to visit.) It was also customary to visit one's friends briefly but formally upon one's return

Chapter 31

Emma believes herself to be in love with Frank Churchill, and wonders how much. She will not accept him if he proposes—and after reading his letter to Mrs Weston, in which he asks her to say goodbye to Harriet

Smith for him, Emma wonders if Harriet might succeed her in his affections.

Mr Elton's wedding is soon to take place. Harriet is very unhappy, and Emma appeals to her to stop brooding on it for her sake. Harriet is all affection and regret; Emma thinks what a splendid, warm-hearted wife she would make, perhaps to Frank Churchill when she herself refuses him.

Chapter 32

Mr Elton brings his new wife home, and Emma takes Harriet to pay her their formal visit. Harriet thinks she is charming; Emma is more critical, considering her vain, self-satisfied, and either foolish or ignorant. When she returns the visit she declares herself enchanted by Hartfield, because it is just like Maple Grove, the house of her rich brother-in-law Mr Suckling. Her conversation is self-centred and full of clichés. She advises Emma to go to Bath for her father's health and her own social prospects: she discusses her own intense love of music, Mrs Weston (whom she is surprised to discover is a gentlewoman though she has been a governess), and Mr Knightley (whom she considers 'quite the gentleman'). Emma is disgusted by her pretentiousness; Mr Woodhouse thinks her pleasant.

NOTES AND GLOSSARY:

visits in form ... receiving wedding-visits ... pay her respects: it was customary for neighbours to pay a formal visit to a new wife in her new home. Later in the chapter, 'not to wait upon a bride is very remiss'

when the visit was returned: the new wife then had to repay the visit by calling upon everyone who had called on her. Dinner parties were also arranged in honour of the newly united couple (Emma holds one in Chapter 34)

barouche-landau: a four-wheeled carriage which can be driven closed or open, in which two couples can sit facing each other

the very person for you to go into public with ... going into public under the auspices of a friend of Mrs Elton's ... who, with the help of a boarder, just made a shift to live: as young ladies could not be seen in public alone, they often stayed with a paid chaperone who would 'launch' them in society

I condition for nothing else: that is all I insist on

in so regular a train: in so well organised a routine

'Knightley': Mrs Elton is eager to show familiarity by using Mr Knightley's surname without the 'Mr', and by doing so shows her vulgarity—the form is particularly unsuitable for a woman to use. Emma herself calls him 'Mr Knightley' although she has known him for a long time

my *caro sposo*: *(Italian)* a vulgar and affected way of referring to her 'dear husband'

nice: fastidious

a bride . . . is always the first in company, let the others be who they may: it was (and still is, in some parts of society) the custom to allow the new wife to precede everyone in entering a room or going in to dinner—even those who would normally have precedence over her. Mrs Elton is also given the honour of starting the first dance at the ball (Chapter 38)

Chapter 33

Emma finds no reason to revise her low opinion of Mrs Elton, but Mr Elton seems proud of her, and the neighbourhood praises her. Mrs Elton, sensing Emma's dislike, changes from her original intimate manner towards her and becomes colder. She is rude to Harriet, but likes and praises Jane Fairfax to excess, and plans to encourage and invite her, and to introduce her to her own friends. Jane Fairfax stays on in Highbury, although the Campbells invite her to join them in Ireland; Emma wonders what prevents her from going, and imagines a 'decree' forbidding her to see Mr Dixon, especially as in Highbury she is thrown into the company of Mrs Elton, which Emma finds deplorable. Mr Knightley points out that she is at the mercy of Mrs Elton because nobody else (including Emma) pays her such attention. Emma probes Mr Knightley about his marrying Jane Fairfax: he denies the possibility, saying that she has not the 'open temper' he would wish for in a wife. She is too reserved–even more so than she used to be. Emma thinks his statement is conclusive; Mrs Weston is not so sure.

NOTES AND GLOSSARY:

It was not to be doubted . . . conjugal unreserve: he had certainly told Mrs Elton about Harriet's love for him, thus keeping the rule that husbands and wives should tell each other everything. (This notion recurs with reference to Harriet's attachment to Mr Knightley, which Emma does not feel free to reveal to him even after their engagement, in Chapter 53)

'Full many a flower . . . desert air': From Thomas Gray's (1716–71) *Elegy in a Country Churchyard* (1750). 'Fragrance' should be 'sweetness'
sensibilities: sensitivity (of taste and of emotion)
do not beat me: do not contend with me

Chapter 34

Social duty compels Emma to give a dinner party for the newly married Eltons. She invites Jane Fairfax because Mr Knightley's reproach has made her realise she does not offer her enough friendship. Mr John Knightley unexpectedly attends, and remarks to Miss Fairfax that he has seen her walking in the rain; she replies that she walks to the post office every day and they exchange pleasantries about the attraction of the post office and letters from friends. Her future position as governess, she says sadly, will prevent her from being close to her friends; he hopes that she will be living among those she loves. Mr Woodhouse is shocked to hear that she has been walking in the rain; Jane Fairfax refuses all offers to have her letters collected for her. Emma refrains from hinting about the Irish post; she is sure from Jane Fairfax's happier look that she has received a letter from Mr Dixon. She is determined to be more friendly to Jane Fairfax. On mentioning Frank Churchill's name, she realises that she is not disturbed, therefore cannot be seriously in love with him.

NOTES AND GLOSSARY:
rout-cakes: rich cakes usually served at receptions; Mrs Elton finds them inferior
ice: here ice-cream
not sitting at the bottom of the table himself: not presiding at the table—which as host it was his duty to do
opposed to her: sitting opposite to her
I always fetch the letters . . . It saves trouble: The post office did not deliver letters to people's houses. Jane Fairfax says that she collects the letters to save anyone else the trouble of doing so
concentrated objects: objects of affection gathered closely around
you sad girl: you silly girl
boys have very little teaching after an early age: boys do not go on learning handwriting at home because they go away to boarding school
if I were very bad: Emma means that if she were in a very acute state of love for Frank Churchill she would be unable to speak his name calmly in public

must I go first?: Mrs Elton is over-eager, ready to go first in to dinner before she is asked to do so: she also takes the honour of going first as if it were personal to her, and not merely due to her position as the most recently married woman (see note to Chapter 32)

Chapter 35

After dinner Mrs Elton monopolises Jane Fairfax and discusses her future, undertaking to find her a 'situation' as governess quickly—against Jane Fairfax's wishes. Mr Weston arrives with a letter from Frank Churchill announcing that, as the Churchills will be in London, he will soon be able to come back to Highbury. The Westons are delighted and Emma is full of delightful agitation, but Mr Woodhouse and Mr Knightley are less pleased.

NOTES AND GLOSSARY:

the slave-trade ... abolition: Mrs Elton is talking about the controversy over trading in slave labour, abolished in 1807. Jane Fairfax sees 'governess-trade' as equally inhumane

put it up: put it away

Chapter 36

Mr Weston and Mrs Elton discuss Frank Churchill's arrival, the journey from Yorkshire, Mrs Churchill's health and, of course, Maple Grove. Mr John Knightley is leaving his sons to stay with the Woodhouses—he wonders if in view of all the social activity current in Highbury, Emma will have too many engagements to look after them. Mr Knightley offers to have them. Emma argues that she has few social engagements; that he himself is present at the same ones; that she is hardly away from home for more than an hour whereas he is; and at home he is always 'either reading to himself or settling his accounts'. This amuses him greatly.

NOTES AND GLOSSARY:

She means to sleep only two nights on the road: she will stay only two nights at an inn on her journey

a retired place: a secluded place

a certain gentleman: she is referring coyly to Mr Elton

Hymen's saffron robe: from *L'Allegro*, a poem by John Milton (1608–74): 'let Hymen oft appear/In saffron robe'. Hymen is the God of marriage. She means 'before we married'

tea was carrying round: tea was being carried round

wanting notice: lacking attention
do not physic them: do not give them medicine

Chapter 37

Emma reflects on Frank Churchill's projected visit; she feels she is not really in love with him, but fancies that he is in love with her. She resolves neither to encourage him nor to let him declare his love. When he arrives she is pleased to observe that he seems less in love with her than before. He is restless and leaves after a quarter of an hour—she wonders if he is afraid of her power to revive his love. His stay is brief, and he does not visit Highbury again for ten days, as his aunt's health requires that he stay in London with the Churchills. They decide, however, to take a house in Richmond, only nine miles away, so Highbury may see more of him, and the ball becomes a possibility again.

NOTES AND GLOSSARY:
the Enscombe family: the family from Enscombe (the Churchills)

Chapter 38

The ball takes place. Frank Churchill seems restless again, especially when the Eltons' carriage arrives—they have forgotten the Bateses, but send their carriage back for them. Miss Bates is voluble in her praise of everything: the arrangements, the food, the dresses. Mrs Elton chats to Jane Fairfax. The Westons decide that Mrs Elton must be the first lady to dance as she is the most recently married—which annoys Emma, who considers the ball as specially for her. She dances with Frank Churchill, and is pleased that he seems more a friend than a lover. She is sorry that Mr Knightley does not dance—he looks so distinguished. Mr Elton snubs Harriet cruelly: when she is the only young lady not dancing, he does not ask her to dance, and even refuses when Mrs Weston asks him to do so—a very public insult. To Emma's delight, Mr Knightley saves Harriet from embarrassment by asking her to dance. He and Emma discuss Mr Elton's rudeness, and in return for Emma's acknowledgement that she has misjudged Mr Elton, Mr Knightley admits that Harriet would have been preferable to Mrs Elton. He asks Emma with whom she is going to dance—and she says 'with you, if you will ask me'; they agree that they are not so much 'brother and sister' as to make it improper.

NOTES AND GLOSSARY:
privy counsellors: inner advisers to a king
Aladdin's lamp: the fairytale character Aladdin had a lamp which when rubbed would produce anything he wished for

wedding-present: here, a present given by the bride to her friends and attendants
an olive: an olive-coloured shawl
the respectable length of the set as it was forming: enough pairs of dancers were getting up to dance, in formation together, to make a long double line. Later, when Harriet is flying 'farther down the middle', she and her partner are dancing between the two facing lines formed by the other couples
tippet: a scarf, probably of fur
conversable: easy to talk to

Chapter 39

In her reflections after the ball, Emma rejoices that she and Mr Knightley agree about the Eltons; that Frank Churchill is not too much in love with her; and that Mr Elton's rudeness has at last cured Harriet of her infatuation with him. Frank Churchill has said he is leaving Highbury, so she is surprised to see him arrive with Harriet, who faints as soon as she reaches the house. She has been badly frightened, when walking with a friend, by gipsies who have threatened and surrounded her. Her friend has run away, and Frank Churchill, on his way to return a pair of scissors to Miss Bates, has come upon her surrounded by gipsies and rescued her. It strikes Emma that this accident may have been fortunate in throwing Harriet and Frank Churchill together—though she resolves not to interfere. Mr Woodhouse is most disturbed by the misadventure.

NOTES AND GLOSSARY:
sweepgate: the gate at the entrance to the drive
imaginist: someone who imagines things—a good description of Emma

Chapter 40

Harriet comes to Emma with a small parcel labelled 'most precious treasures'. She is going to destroy her mementoes of Mr Elton—some sticking-plaster that was left over when he bound a cut finger, and one of his old pencils. She burns them, saying 'there is an end, thank Heaven! of Mr Elton', and Emma wonders when there will be 'a beginning of Mr Churchill'. Two weeks later, Harriet announces that she will never marry. Emma asks if she thinks the person she loves is out of her reach, and Harriet talks of the 'infinite superiority to the rest of the world' of somebody to whom she feels grateful. Emma, thinking she means Frank

Churchill, spurs her on to think that 'more wonderful things have taken place, there have been matches of great disparity'. She congratulates her on her good taste, and feels that an attachment to Frank Churchill will tend to 'raise and refine' Harriet's mind.

NOTES AND GLOSSARY:

court plaister: silk sticking-plaster

spruce beer: beer made from the leaves and small branches of the spruce tree

***told* no fortune:** gipsies were supposed to be able to (fore)tell one's future, or 'fortune'

the service he rendered you: this is the key to the misunderstanding between Harriet, who feels 'gratitude, wonder and veneration' towards Mr Knightley for rescuing her from Mr Elton's cruelty at the ball, and Emma, who is referring to Frank Churchill's 'service' in rescuing Harriet from the gipsies

Chapter 41

Jane Fairfax is still at Highbury as the Campbells are still in Ireland. Mr Knightley begins to detect signs of an 'understanding' between her and Frank Churchill, whom he detests. Frank Churchill mentions that Mr Perry, the doctor, is going to get a carriage, a fact that has only been told in confidence to the Bateses and Jane Fairfax. Mr Knightley detects some confusion in Frank Churchill, who says he has had a dream about the carriage; but Jane Fairfax betrays nothing. Frank Churchill proposes a game with alphabet letters; he makes the word 'blunder' for Jane Fairfax, who blushes and conceals it, though Mr Knightley sees it; then the word 'Dixon' for Emma, asking her if he should show it to Miss Fairfax. He does so: she is displeased and leaves quickly with her aunt. Mr Knightley feels it his duty to speak to Emma about this last word and why it embarrassed Miss Fairfax. Has she not noticed signs of attachment between her and Frank Churchill? Emma confidently assures him that he is mistaken. He is irritated by her gaiety and curiosity on the subject—and also by Mr Woodhouse's hot fire on such a warm night.

NOTES AND GLOSSARY:

Mr Knightley . . . began to suspect: this is the first time we see 'inside' Mr Knightley's mind

'Myself creating what I saw': from a long poem, *The Task*, by William Cowper (1731–1800). Mr Knightley, unless he is imagining things, sees suspicious behaviour

setting up his carriage: getting, and making arrangements for the upkeep of, a carriage

the small-sized Pembroke: a small table with two side-flaps which can be raised

Chapter 42

To take the place of an expedition planned by the Westons and the Eltons to Box Hill, postponed because of a lame carriage horse, Mr Knightley proposes a visit to his house, Donwell Abbey, to taste his famous strawberries. Mrs Elton wishes to take charge of the inviting and arranging, but he insists on doing it himself. At this handsome house with its beautiful park, Emma reflects how fortunate it is that Isabella's marriage to Mr John Knightley has linked the Woodhouses to true gentility, and nobility of blood and mind.

After they have picked strawberries, Mrs Elton tells Jane Fairfax that she has found her a situation as governess, and refuses to believe that she does not want to take it; finally Jane Fairfax asks Mr Knightley to show them the magnificent gardens, with their avenue of lime trees, vistas, woods and river. As Mr Knightley is discussing agricultural methods with Harriet, Emma has few fears that she will think of Robert Martin, whose house can be seen on the estate. Frank Churchill is expected, but still has not come. Jane Fairfax leaves hastily and in distress, telling Emma that her spirits are exhausted but refusing her carriage; Emma pities her. Frank Churchill arrives hot, agitated and out of humour. He says he wants to travel and leave England. He agrees to join the party to Box Hill the next day.

NOTES AND GLOSSARY:

Box Hill: a beauty spot in the south of England, very popular for picnic parties

timber which neither fashion nor extravagance had rooted up: Donwell still had its 'rows and avenues' of trees because they had not been removed to suit the fashionable taste in landscape gardening, nor had they had to be sold as timber to pay the owners' debts

Chapter 43

The picnic party to Box Hill starts badly. Frank Churchill is dull at first, then gay and talkative, devoting his attention to Emma, who responds playfully. Their banter lays them open to the charge of flirting: Frank Churchill is over-gallant and the rest of the party is shocked at their easy talk. Frank Churchill pretends that Emma wants each of them to say one very clever thing, two moderately clever things, or 'three things very dull indeed', and when Miss Bates good-humouredly replies that she is sure to say three dull things, Emma most unkindly counters with 'There may be a difficulty. Pardon me, but you will be limited as to number—only three at once'. Carried away by Frank Churchill's mood, Emma has overstepped the bounds of playfulness. Miss Bates is hurt; Mr Knightley is grave; the Eltons walk away. Frank Churchill remarks that they were lucky to marry so successfully after knowing each other for only a few weeks in Bath. Jane Fairfax comments that many such attachments are formed, but they can be severed. Frank Churchill jokingly asks Emma to choose a wife for him, and she immediately thinks of Harriet. Even she eventually tires of his excessive high spirits, which jar with the peaceful scenery they have come to enjoy. Mr Knightley reproaches Emma for her insensitive rudeness to Miss Bates.

Chapter 44

Emma is contrite as she recalls her unkindness to Miss Bates. She visits the Bateses to make amends; Miss Bates is grateful and almost herself, but Jane Fairfax will not see her. She is not well. She has accepted the place as governess that Mrs Elton has found, and is to leave in two weeks. To Emma's surprise, Frank Churchill has left Highbury. She contrasts Mrs Churchill's importance in the world with Jane Fairfax's insignificance, and feels that her speculations about Jane Fairfax and the piano have been both fanciful and unfair.

NOTES AND GLOSSARY:

John ostler: John, the stableman at the inn

Chapter 45

Mr Knightley unexpectedly announces that he is going to London. He shows his approval when Mr Woodhouse tells him that Emma has called on the Bateses. News comes that Mrs Churchill has died—to everyone's surprise, as she was not considered to be really ill. Emma wonders how her death will affect Frank Churchill—will he now, without fear of Mrs Churchill's opposition, form an attachment to Harriet and marry her? Emma resolves to be more affectionate to Jane Fairfax and invites her to spend a day at Hartfield—but she declines because of illness. She also refuses Emma's invitation to drive out in her carriage, and even sends back an offering of invalid food. Emma at last realises that Miss Fairfax does not wish to accept kindnesses from her; her sadness is lessened by the thought that Mr Knightley at least would approve of her kind intentions.

Chapter 46

Mrs Weston sends Mr Weston to request Emma to visit her. When she hears that Frank Churchill has visited them, she guesses that the news that is to be broken to her is to do with him, and thinks 'first of herself and then of Harriet'. To her astonishment, Mrs Weston's news is that Frank Churchill and Jane Fairfax are engaged to be married, and have been since the previous October when they were at Weymouth with the Campbells. Mrs Weston is worried lest Frank's attentions to Emma have led her to believe that he loves her; she is relieved when Emma reassures her that the liking she had for him is long past. Emma is privately outraged, mentally criticising the couple for their secrecy, which has misled everybody, and blaming Frank Churchill for allowing Jane to be engaged as a governness. Mrs Weston says that the couple had had misunderstandings, and that it is Jane Fairfax's engagement as a governess that has forced Frank Churchill to tell Mr Churchill everything. Without the domineering Mrs Churchill to object, he has been given permission to marry. Emma is particularly upset at the thought of what she has said to Frank Churchill about Jane Fairfax and Mr Dixon. The Westons are resigned to the match, though it is not materially a good one for Frank; Emma offers her congratulations, and they all begin to be reconciled to the idea.

NOTES AND GLOSSARY:

the late event at Richmond: Mrs Churchill's death

cut off: she imagines dreadful news: that Mrs Churchill had six 'natural' or illegitimate children to whom she has left Frank's inheritance

'the world is not theirs, nor the world's law': an adaptation of a phrase in Dr Johnson's (1709–84) magazine, *The Rambler*, taken from *Romeo and Juliet* by William Shakespeare: 'The world is not their friend, nor the world's law'. Emma is pitying friendless women, and Jane Fairfax

Chapter 47

Emma feels guilty and remorseful for having encouraged Harriet to care for Frank Churchill. Yet again she has misled her and made her hope for a match out of her reach. Now she must again tell Harriet news that will distress her. Harriet has, however, heard the 'secret' from Mr Weston, and Emma is amazed by her calmness. She asks how this can be, when Harriet has implied that she cares for Frank Churchill who rescued her from the gipsies, and Harriet in equal astonishment replies that she has been talking about Mr Knightley, who rescued her at the ball. Emma has encouraged her to think that she can marry her social superior; to Emma's alarm and dismay, she believes that Mr Knightley returns her affection. Now Emma at last sees the truth—'it darted through her, with the speed of an arrow, that Mr Knightley must marry no one but herself!' She does not know when she first loved him; she has been totally ignorant of her own heart.

Emma goes through another period of self-analysis and self-disgust. She has arrogantly arranged other people's affairs, has been 'universally mistaken', and has done wrong to Harriet, to herself, and probably to Mr Knightley. She alone has been responsible for this connection, so 'unequal' in rank, in ability, in intelligence. Emma reproaches herself for bringing Harriet forward in society, for discouraging her from marrying Robert Martin—and above all for giving her presumptuous ideas.

NOTES AND GLOSSARY:

such an engrossing charge: a responsibility taking up all her attention

Chapter 48

Emma realises that she has always wished to be first with Mr Knightley—a position she has undeservedly filled for many years. He has encouraged and advised her, reproached her justly and tried to improve her. She wishes him never to marry, and herself never to marry—even if he were to ask her. She suggests to Harriet that they do not meet in private for a while.

Mrs Weston has called on Jane Fairfax who has told her how wretched she has felt during the months of her secret engagement, and how guilty she feels for her ungraciousness to Emma. Emma realises that she should have made friends not with Harriet but with Jane Fairfax, who was her equal in social rank, ability and education. Instead, her speculation and gossiping to Frank about Mr Dixon, and their flirtatiousness, have given great pain to Jane Fairfax.

The weather is cold and wet; Mr Woodhouse is not well; Emma feels that her circle of friends is about to dissolve. Mrs Weston is to have a child, Frank Churchill and Jane Fairfax will leave, and if Mr Knightley is no longer her friend but Harriet's husband, she will have no companions—all through her own fault. Her only consolation is her own resolution to become more rational, and to know herself better.

Chapter 49

Mr Knightley returns suddenly from London and asks Emma to walk with him. After a silence, Emma mentions the wedding of Frank

Churchill and Jane Fairfax; he has already heard of it from Mr Weston. Emma says she has been 'blind' about it. He is very sympathetic, believing that she loves Frank Churchill; she explains that she does not care for him, and that the engagement has not hurt her. Mr Knightley thinks Frank Churchill is fortunate in his marriage; he wishes to tell Emma why he envies him, but she, fearing a revelation about Harriet, asks him not to speak. He is hurt. Emma thinks she has been unkind and says he can speak to her as a friend: he speaks with love and asks if he can hope to succeed with *her*. To her amazed happiness, he reveals that he loves her: within half an hour, Mr Knightley, who has only come to console her about Frank Churchill, has passed from misery to happiness, and so has she. He had always been jealous of Frank Churchill and went to London 'to learn to be indifferent'. Emma has been afraid he loved Harriet. Now each has 'the precious certainty of being beloved'.

NOTES AND GLOSSARY:

she was his own Emma, by hand and word: she had promised him her hand in marriage, and she had pledged herself to him by word

Chapter 50

Emma is happy—but she feels a great sense of responsibility towards her father, and towards Harriet. She will never leave her father, so can only be engaged to Mr Knightley; her worries about Harriet are more difficult to resolve. She does not wish to cause her pain, and feels unable to meet her: she will ask Isabella to invite her to London.

A note arrives from Mrs Weston enclosing a very long letter she has received from Frank Churchill. He explains his conduct and justifies it by the necessity of keeping his engagement secret from Mr and Mrs Churchill. He apologises above all for his behaviour towards Emma, but feels she was not misled by his attentions, and may even have guessed his secret. He admits to having visited Highbury only when Jane Fairfax was there. He explains some of the mysteries: it was he who ordered the piano, unknown to Jane; he arrived out of temper at Donwell because he had met Jane, who had refused to let him walk with her; he neglected her and showed 'apparent devotion' to Emma the next day at Box Hill because of his resentment. He left Highbury because he had quarrelled with Jane, and she took the job as governess because he had not posted his reply to her letter breaking their engagement. Now they are reconciled; and he ends: 'If you think me in a way to be happier than I deserve, I am quite of your opinion.'

NOTES AND GLOSSARY:

the event of the 26th ult: Mrs Churchill's death—also described as 'the late event', below

Chapter 51

This letter makes Emma think Frank Churchill is 'less than she had supposed': he is grateful to Mrs Weston, repentant and in love, so she, in her happiness, cannot judge him severely. Mr Knightley criticises him for his flattery, for his secrecy, for his behaviour, and especially for causing unnecessary suffering to Jane Fairfax, whom he should have been protecting. Being married to her will, however, improve him.

Mr Knightley discusses with Emma how he can marry her without causing unhappiness to her father, whom she feels she can never leave: he will come and live at Hartfield instead of Donwell as long as her father is alive—a great sacrifice for him, thinks Emma, and a great comfort for her.

Now all that spoils Emma's happiness is the thought of Harriet who must be 'a loser in every way'—she must be kept at a distance from them to spare her feelings. Emma fears that Harriet will never fall out of love with Mr Knightley, or easily find a successor to him.

Chapter 52

Harriet is to stay with Isabella in London for a fortnight. Now Emma can enjoy Mr Knightley's visits without feeling guilty about her. She has not yet told her father of her engagement. She calls on Jane Fairfax who is welcoming, animated and pretty. Mrs Elton drops many hints about the engagement; Mr Elton arrives cross, having missed Mr Knightley at Donwell. Jane Fairfax and Emma speak warmly to each other, the former apologising for her misconduct in having a secret engagement. She is to be married as soon as the period of mourning for Mrs Churchill is over, in three months.

NOTES AND GLOSSARY:

ridicule: reticule, small mesh bag

'For when a lady's in the case': from *Fables, The Hare and Many Friends* by John Gay (1685–1732)

stand at our sideboard: be our butler (who stood supervising the dining-room while the other servants waited at table)

'three months of deep mourning': there were different stages in mourning the death of a relative. During 'deep mourning' one wore black, and could not have festivities such as weddings

Chapter 53

Mrs Weston gives birth to a daughter, and Emma and Mr Knightley wonder if she will educate her daughter as she did Emma. Both laughingly acknowledge Emma's faults, her improvement, and Mr Knightley's influence on her; he says he has loved her since she was thirteen (and he thirty). She has always called him Mr Knightley and will continue to do so. She regrets that she must in delicacy keep one secret from him—Harriet's feelings for him. Isabella writes that Harriet has recovered her spirits in London. Mr John Knightley writes to congratulate his brother, and, surprisingly, says that the news of his engagement is not unexpected.

Emma tells her father that she and Mr Knightley intend to marry; he is shocked and upset, though he likes and relies on Mr Knightley; he wants everything to continue as it is. He eventually agrees to the idea of marriage—in a year or two. Mrs Weston thinks the match suitable in every way; Mr Weston tells the Bateses and the news spreads to everyone; all approve except the Eltons, who pity Mr Knightley.

NOTES AND GLOSSARY:

'like La Baronne d'Almane ou La Comtesse d'Ostalis, in Madame de Genlis' Adelaide and Theodore: *Adelaide and Theodore* is the name of the English translation (1783) of a book by the famous French educational theorist, Madame de Genlis (1746–1830)

in the building in which N. takes M. for better, for worse: in the church. Emma is referring to the wedding service, which is set out in the prayer-book with these initials where the couple say their names

Chapter 54

Mr Knightley tells Emma some news: Harriet Smith is to marry Robert Martin, whom she has met again in London when he had to take some papers there for Mr Knightley. Emma professes herself satisfied with the match, and Mr Knightley remarks that she has changed since they last discussed the subject; she admits that she was a fool then. He says that he too has changed: he has revised his opinion of Harriet in talking to her, and thinks her amiable, of good principles and suited to 'domestic life'. The news of Harriet's marriage and happiness relieves Emma, who can now tell Mr Knightley everything. They meet Jane Fairfax and Frank Churchill at the Westons'; Emma and Frank, despite 'a number of embarrassing recollections on each side', speak kindly and forgivingly to each other—then he teases her by saying 'Dixon'. Emma accuses him of having had some amusement out of misleading everyone—something which she *might* have enjoyed herself. She thinks they are a little alike—they are alike too in marrying people superior to themselves in character. He reminds her of 'Mr Perry's carriage': Jane wonders how he can bear to recollect such painful things. Emma reflects on Mr Knightley's superiority of character over Frank Churchill.

NOTES AND GLOSSARY:

Astley's: a place of entertainment resembling a circus, the *Royal Amphitheatre* founded in 1798 by Philip Astley (1742–1814), an equestrian performer

Chapter 55

Emma congratulates Harriet when she returns, a little shamefaced about her change of heart, but truly happy about her engagement to Robert Martin. Her parentage becomes known. She is the illegitimate daughter of a tradesman, rich and decent, but by no means of 'the blood of gentility' which Emma had imagined for her. The connection with Mr Knightley or with Frank Churchill would have been most unsuitable. In marrying Robert Martin she will find 'security, stability and improvement'. Her intimacy with the Martins will gradually and naturally efface her friendship with Emma.

Harriet and Robert Martin are to be married by Mr Elton in October. Jane Fairfax returns to the Campbells, Frank Churchill to his uncle, and they wait for November for their wedding. Emma and Mr Knightley choose October, but Mr Woodhouse is not happy, feeling himself neglected. When Mrs Weston's poultry-yard is robbed of all its turkeys, Mr Woodhouse feels he needs the protection of Mr Knightley, and he gives his consent. Mr Elton performs the ceremony, which Mrs Elton considers too modest: but the wishes and hopes of their true friends come true in the perfect happiness of their marriage.

Part 3

Commentary

Subject and scope

The message

Emma is a close study of a small circle of people and their relationships with each other, exposed in ironic detail. Emma herself as the central character holds our interest, but it is her relationships with other people that are the outward and visible signs of her inward development. If the novel has a lesson, it is that one cannot alter society, and should not try to do so (as Emma does in her manipulation of other people). Within Jane Austen's general theme that one should see real life without being blinded by romantic notions, literary expectations, pride, prejudice or 'fancy', is the central motif of *Emma*: 'knows thyself'. Emma can accommodate herself to her society only by seeing it clearly and by seeing herself clearly, with all her flaws and fantasies. The development of the novel is a progression towards self-knowledge.

The social setting

Forms

Because society is not merely a setting, but an integral part of the novel, the social forms are of particular significance. According to the characters' awareness of them, we are given details of everyday rituals such as tea, dinner, Emma's purchase of a commodious circular table to seat enough people; the forms of card-parties, dinner-parties, picnic parties and balls are charted for us (we notice, for example, details such as the fact that the less important guests are invited to the Coles' after the more important ones have dined). We observe the polite course of visiting one's friends formally on arrival in a district, and before leaving; the special procedures for visiting and inviting a newly married woman, allowing her to lead in to dinner, and to be the first to dance. The observance of custom matters greatly: to go against the carefully established ritual built up over the centuries can harm or hurt or disturb. Frank Churchill's secret engagement to Jane Fairfax, for example, puts everyone in a false position; Highbury is belittled, Emma is duped, Jane Fairfax is distressed. Emma's 'humiliations' are usually the result of her disregard for the normal observances of society: she speaks rudely to an inferior (Miss Bates); makes friends with an inferior (Harriet); and is too outspoken with a member of the opposite sex (Frank Churchill) in private and in public (shocking the party at Box Hill). She is also guilty of trying to push Harriet into two marriages above her station, and out of a conventional and appropriate one to Robert Martin.

Rank and money

The social spectrum of *Emma*, as is usual in Jane Austen's novels, is narrow: we see simply a small subsection of the middle class. The point that Jane Austen is making about class is that within even a tiny section of society, everyone is extremely conscious of where they are (or wish to be) and of whom they consider below them. Mrs Elton's background in trade, for example, is very suspect, and her position is redeemed only by her money.

There are no noble or aristocratic people in this novel. Mr and Mrs Churchill are considered grand, though they have no title; Frank Churchill is bettering himself by living with them and taking their name. Mr Knightley is the elder son of a rich, landowning family, so he has inherited the estate of Donwell Abbey—its lands, farms and house, and most of the money to keep the estate going. Younger sons had a limited choice of profession, often the army or the Church; Mr Knightley's brother John earns his own money, as a lawyer, respectably but not grandly. Emma and her father are considered 'first in consequence' in Highbury but own much less land than Mr Knightley; we do not know if her father is really rich, and he is certainly not of titled family. Mr and Mrs Weston are moderately well-to-do: he has money to keep them comfortably, but apart from a small independent income, and marriage to a rich first wife, he too has had to earn the money on which they now live. Mrs Weston has not been at all wealthy, having had to make her way as a governess, the fate dreaded by Jane Fairfax. The Coles, we hear, have also been 'in trade' and are now rich enough to entertain; Emma snobbishly considers refusing their invitation for that very reason.

Mr and Miss Bates have neither rank nor money and are Emma's social inferiors, as Mr Knightley points out. Jane Fairfax is the daughter of an army officer: she must earn her own living because even her benefactors, the Campbells, have not the money to support her once she is grown up. It is very likely that Mr Elton was also a younger son, who became a clergyman not because of a religious vocation but as a means of earning a living (he seems to have no religious preoccupations or occupations, apart from performing the marriage ceremonies). Clergymen were not well paid; he had to marry prudently, and did well financially to marry Mrs Elton, 'with so many thousands as would always be called ten', thus assuring himself of a comfortable income, though the undignified object in which her family traded is tactfully not mentioned.

Robert Martin is a tenant farmer; not a peasant, but a 'gentleman farmer' who rents a house and land on Mr Knightley's estate. Despite Emma's scathing remarks about the impossibility of her having a farmer's wife for a friend, he is respectable if modest in rank, probably, as Emma says, putting his money into stock for his farm; he is neither poor nor of the lower class.

Harriet's position is anomalous; as Emma sees, her illegitimacy would have been little handicap had she been the daughter of a titled person; as the daughter of a decent tradesman, the romance of rank can no longer be attached to her.

The servant class only comes into the novel as meals, furniture or trees do—that is, when a character is aware of them. Mr Woodhouse is about as considerate of James his coachman as he is of the horses. They do not count in the social structure, nor in the novel—in fact, Emma teases Mr Knightley for his interest in and reliance on William Larkins.

It is clear that money is not equivalent to wealth, though it may buy some of its privileges. One can be wealthy but vulgar like Mrs Elton, or poor but well born like Jane Fairfax. The aim at all times is to be 'genteel' or gentlemanly—to have the appearance and behaviour of one who is well born.

The position of women

It is clear from *Emma* and from other nineteenth-century novels that the young woman's task in life is to get herself as 'well' married as she can, in the financial and/or the social sense. Although Jane Austen wrote to her niece Fanny 'Anything is to be preferred or endured rather than marrying without affection', many women would have felt quite seriously that it was worth marrying any man of sufficient rank and wealth. It was permissible for a woman, through her beauty, to be sought in marriage by a man of higher rank; it was frowned on for a woman to marry beneath her. Once married, she was expected to have a large family. Jane Austen's letters are illuminating on this point. She considered that too much childbearing exhausted women in early life, writing of a friend 'Poor animal, she will be worn out before she is thirty', and telling her niece Fanny not to marry young because 'by not beginning the business of mothering quite so early in life, you will be young in constitution, spirits, figure and countenance'.

Most young women lived with their families until they married. For those whose parents were dead, or not rich enough to support them, there were very few possibilities. Unless she were from the lower class, a woman who had to support herself could not without great stigma and scandal work in a shop, or become a nurse, actress or dancer.

Universities did not admit women, nor were there women lawyers or doctors. 'Secretaries', in a somewhat different capacity from today's, were men. This is the reason why so many women (an estimated forty per cent of unmarried women) became governesses. They were housed, fed, and paid a pittance. Although they lived with the family, they did not necessarily eat or sit with them, and might be treated little better than servants, though their rank and education might be equal to those of their employers. (Mrs Elton tells Jane Fairfax that if only she played the harp, she would be sure to be well treated: 'Your musical knowledge alone would entitle you to name your own terms, have as many rooms as you like, and mix in the family as much as you chose'.) A governess would find her job through personal recommendation, through advertisements in a newspaper, or through an agency ('governess-trade' resembled the slave trade, according to Jane Fairfax). Her duties were to teach the children from when they left their nurses' care until the boys went to a tutor or boarding school, and the girls were about seventeen. She taught the little ones reading, writing and simple arithmetic, and the older girls sewing, painting, music, and whatever languages she knew, usually French. A few governesses might be as lucky as Mrs Weston and stay on when their charges grew up; most had to move on from family to family.

Other positions that a well-brought-up woman could take were those of 'companion' to an older woman, or living-in teacher in a boarding school (not considered very respectable for those of gentle birth). Widows of small means could, like Mrs Elton's friend, take in young ladies whom they would introduce into society for a fee, or act as paid chaperones.

In *Emma*, we see women in a variety of roles. Isabella has done what was expected of her in marrying Mr John Knightley; although only in her twenties, she already has five children. By announcing that she has 'very little intention of ever marrying at all' (Chapter 10), Emma is stepping out of the expected line of a woman's duty. But because she is rich (and will inherit money from her father) she can afford this eccentricity. 'I have none of the usual inducements of women to marry', she says, adding 'Fortune I do not want [lack]; employment I do not want; consequence I do not want'. As she herself points out, there is a great difference between a rich spinster and a poor one such as Miss Bates: 'It is poverty only which makes celibacy contemptible to a generous public. A single woman with a very narrow income must be a ridiculous, disagreeable old maid . . . but a single woman of good fortune is always respectable, and may be as sensible and pleasant as anybody else'. Miss Bates has lived with her mother in cramped and confined apartments all her life, their one servant being the absolute minimum, not a luxury. It is clear that the Bateses exist on the gifts and disguised charity of their friends; their extreme poverty makes Miss Bates's goodness and cheerfulness the more admirable.

Relationships

Relationships of all kinds are very significant in *Emma*, particularly as part of Emma's own development. The relationships which she tries to force fail: Harriet's with Mr Elton and Frank Churchill, or her own with Frank Churchill, which she invents even before she meets him. Where Emma is successful is in close relationships—with her father, her governess, Mr Knightley as a family friend. As Mr Knightley observes, she is much better at dealing with children than with adults because she is 'guided by nature' with children, and not 'under the power of fancy and whim'. The main categories of relationship in the novel could be termed: domestic, familiar, imaginary, deceitful and marital.

Domestic

Emma is skilled in domestic relationships. The affection she inspires in and feels for Isabella, Mrs Weston and her father is remarkable. Even at her most downcast, she knows that she cannot be accused of being a bad daughter. After the misery of being reproached by Mr Knightley at Box Hill for her heartlessness to Miss Bates, she gains some solace from 'giving up the sweetest hours of the twenty-four to her father's comfort'. With respect to him, she cannot be 'open to any severe reproach. As a daughter, she hoped she was not without a heart'. Nor is hers an unthinking affection; she is continually considering him, and working on her relationship with him; she supports his spirits, changes the conversation whenever she feels he is upset, distracts him and amuses him, all with clear-sighted tolerance. One must admire her management of his house, running it exactly as he wishes, but also giving their friends what she feels they wish: he offers them gruel, a *little* tart, *no* custard, and diluted wine; she contrives to supply her visitors 'in a much more satisfactory style'. On a more serious plane, we even see her determining never to leave her father despite her engagement, thus sacrificing herself and Mr Knightley to her father's domestic happiness. Mr Knightley's decision that they will live at Hartfield during Mr Woodhouse's lifetime perpetuates the sacrifice.

Isabella too is a monument of tact towards Mr Woodhouse. When she stays at Hartfield with her five children (and 'a competent number of nursery-maids'), she takes care of them—but not to the point of annoying her father: 'the ways of Hartfield and the feelings of her father were so respected by Mrs John Knightley, that in spite of maternal solicitude for the immediate enjoyment of her little ones, and for their having instantly all the liberty and attendance, all the eating and drinking, and sleeping and playing, which they could possibly wish for, without the smallest delay, the children were never allowed to be long a disturbance to him, either in themselves, or in any restless attendance on them'.

Mr Woodhouse's attitude towards his daughters is equally affectionate; he may be misguided in his conviction that Isabella is miserable at having left Hartfield; he may be over-indulgent towards Emma, and over-ready to praise everything that she does; but she usually feels that he loves and appreciates her. Her conviction of 'his fond affection and confiding esteem', however, is proof more of her own affection than of his. Selfish as he always is, he can never support or comfort her, as we see in her blackest misery, when she thinks she has lost Mr Knightley to Harriet, and we glimpse the strain her domestic attentions cost her: 'The weather affected Mr Woodhouse, and he could only be kept tolerably comfortable by almost ceaseless attention on his daughter's side, and by exertions which had never cost her half so much before'.

Familiar relationships

The companionable familiarity of Emma's relationship with Mr Knightley is apparent even before we know that she is in love with him. They have known each other since she was a child, and in that specially tender part of the novel after they have declared their love, she recalls herself as a pert child calling him 'George' ('as you made no objection, I never did it again'). Her teasing and his censoriousness ('you hear nothing but truth from me') are a bond between them, as he sees—'I have blamed you, and lectured you, and you have borne it as no other woman in England would have borne it'.

We are told throughout the novel that true love, and suitable marriages, can only be experienced by those of equal rank, equal education, equal intelligence, equal gentility and equal good looks. We notice early on that these two fulfil these conditions. Mr Knightley is the one person who sees through Emma; when he reproaches her for her rudeness to Miss Bates, as betraying her rank and social position by snubbing her, it is not only his outspokenness but her reaction that interests us: first disbelief, then mortification; she is quick to respond and repent. She also imagines him approving of her approaches to Jane Fairfax, however late and unsuccessful. Despite this pupil-teacher relationship, they talk as equals. Like her father she feels him to be part of their family, and long before she admits her love for him likes to feel he is 'near'. When Mr John Knightley replaces him at dinner she feels it 'a sad exchange for herself'. She often relates to him, finding him the most distinguished man in the room, the personification of a gentleman.

The love-story of Mr Knightley and Emma is that of transition from one kind of familiarity (that of family) to another (that of lovers). This is most precisely articulated at the ball: '"Whom are you going to dance with?" asked Mr Knightley. She hesitated a moment and then replied, "With you, if you will ask me."' For once, Emma hesitates on a brink, instead of blundering in. '"Will you?" said he, offering his hand. "Indeed I will. You have shown that you can dance, and you know we are not really so much brother and sister as to make it all improper". "Brother and sister! no, indeed."' This transition between two different kinds of familiarity can be seen too at those moments when his rather stern responsibility for her breaks, and he presses her hand or makes as if to kiss it. Each is reluctant to abandon their fraternal familiarity for an untried relationship as lovers. Emma recognises that she depends on being 'first' with Mr Knightley—she is alarmed at the thought of Jane Fairfax, or any woman, at Donwell, married to Mr Knightley, and making her own close relationship with him impossible. The declaration of his love, making it possible for Emma to acknowledge her own love, is the point of convergence for two people who have been gradually drawing closer, with occasional steps away from each other, throughout the novel.

The only other good 'familiar' relationship in the novel is that of Emma and Mrs Weston, which has been tested over eight years as a 'domestic' relationship. The other familiar rclationships are over-familiar, hasty and not to be encouraged. Mrs Elton, who calls Mr Knightley 'Knightley', and Mr Woodhouse her 'old beau', tries to attach herself instantly to Emma, and, when rebuffed, battens onto Jane Fairfax, taking up her cause uninvited. But the same instant over-familiarity is seen in Emma's relationship with Harriet. Emma decides, the first evening they meet, that '*she* would notice her; she would improve her; she would detach her from her bad acquaintance, and introduce her into good society'; next 'Harriet Smith's intimacy at Hartfield was soon a settled thing'. True familiarity should not be so hasty, but born of years of social intercourse.

Imaginary relationships

'Fancy' is the besetting sin not only of Emma but of Highbury. The whole town mulls over Frank Churchill's handsome letters, buzzes with anticipation over his ever postponed arrival, sympathises quite unnecessarily with his father for losing him to the Churchills. Mrs Weston is an addict—she has plans for Frank Churchill and Emma to marry before they have even met. Not only Emma speculates about the piano that mysteriously arrives for Jane Fairfax: most think it comes from Colonel Campbell; Mrs Weston thinks it comes from Mr Knightley, who she 'fancies' may marry Jane Fairfax. Such fancied relationships are many, and dangerous. Harriet, originally modest and unassuming, becomes, under Emma's tutelage, an expert in the art of inventing relationships. Mr Knightley had only to talk to her in an avuncular way for her to think that 'matches of greater disparity had taken place'. She is, throughout, the victim of fancy. Her one real relationship, with Robert Martin, is pushed firmly into the background, and she is propelled into a series of wholly imaginary affairs. Her manufactured love for Mr Elton is the result of Emma's announcement, before she has met Harriet, that she will find him a wife. Emma never considers Mr Elton's *feelings* for Harriet, merely his *attentions*, which she misinterprets. Nor does she consider Harriet's emotions: to Emma it is merely an exercise in fancy. When Harriet oscillates between Mr Elton and Robert Martin, they seem interchangeable; and later when she and Emma talk at cross purposes about Mr Knightley and Frank Churchill, that very interchangeability shows the impersonality of all 'imaginary relationships'.

It is, however, Emma who is the most dedicated exponent of fancy. We are given a definition and exposition of fancy in Chapter 39, when Frank Churchill rescues Harriet from the gipsies: 'a fine young man and a lovely young woman thrown together in such a way, could hardly fail of suggesting certain ideas to the coldest heart and the steadiest brain'. Here we see the literary basis of fancy; in any romantic story, such an adventure would be bound to end in the marriage of the two protagonists. Emma reflects that even a linguist, a grammarian or a mathematician would have thought that 'circumstances were at work to make them peculiarly interesting to each other'. Emma proudly categorises herself as an 'imaginist': 'How much more must an imaginist, like herself, be on fire with speculation and foresight!—especially with such a ground-work of anticipation as her mind had already made'. Here we have the labours of the imaginist or dealer in fancy—recognition of the romantic moment, on top of a 'groundwork of speculation'. Emma continues to muse on the coincidence; she feels they are ripe for each other; 'He was wishing to get the better of his attachment to herself, she just recovering from her mania for Mr Elton'. Like the children who 'were still asking every day for the story of Harriet and the gipsies', she gloats on the story. We of course have noticed that Frank Churchill, who was meant to be leaving post-haste, was actually going to see the Bateses on the flimsy pretext of returning a pair of scissors.

Emma's idea of love, for herself and for other people, is coloured by her fancy. Inexperienced, she thinks of love in the abstract. She decides that she and Frank Churchill are destined for each other on vague hearsay. This supposing leads her to think that they are in rapport with each other from their very first meeting. Her abstract, fanciful idea of love enables her to believe that he loves her, and also to shift in a moment from loving him to not loving him. Her imagined relationship with him reaches its most uncontrolled point at Box Hill when she allows herself to be openly flattered by him, when she talks to him too familiarly, when she apparently allies herself with him against the rest of the party, and the innocent Miss Bates. It is this lack of control, which is a product of their false relationship, that shocks. They transgress in private as well as in public: by gossiping in such an intimate way about Jane Fairfax, by having private jokes about Mr Dixon, they are breaking the social code.

Despite their animated conversations, they do not 'communicate'. On grounds of fancy, she thinks this opening phrase, 'You cannot be unaware', heralds a proposal to herself, when he is about to reveal his engagement to Jane Fairfax: this would have been a tremendous confidence, the sign of a real, not an imagined relationship. They finally achieve this real friendship when both know real love for someone else.

Deceitful relationships

At the end of the novel everybody is reconciled to the idea of Frank Churchill and Jane Fairfax's engagement. But by keeping it secret they have betrayed their friends and led them into false positions. They meet in a hole-and-corner way, pretending to mend spectacles or to pore over the pianoforte. The pianoforte is a symbol of the destructiveness of deceitful love: kindly meant by him, it exposes Jane Fairfax to gossip and speculation. It is, as Mr Knightley says, wrong to give where the gift can cause harm. Frank Churchill's letters also cause harm: Jane Fairfax's walks to the post office attract notice. It was quite unthinkable for a respectable young lady to have a secret correspondence; their deceitful alliance is making her act in an anti-social way. Emma was in fact correct in her suspicion that something secret was afoot. The effects upon Jane Fairfax of her deceitful relationship are painful. She becomes ill and strained: 'the consciousness of having done amiss, had exposed her to a thousand inquietudes, and made her captious and irritable'. In forcing her to conceal their engagement, that essentially public matter, Frank Churchill is cheating. Public and private should correspond; in making the two so grossly different, he is committing an offence against society.

Marital relationships

There are relatively few married couples in *Emma*. Isabella and Mr John Knightley seem a standard partnership: she bears and looks after children; humours his irritability just as she humoured her father's fractiousness; quietly continues the socialising that she loves despite his destestation of it. There is a hint that the effort is more on her part than on his: she is described as a 'worshipping wife', and Emma, when Mr John Knightley complains about going out to dinner, feels unable to provide the 'Very true, my love' which is Isabella's usual reply to her husband.

There is less difficulty in being a good wife to the easy Mr Weston. He and Mrs Weston are equal in rank, not grand but very respectable; his accumulation of money compensates for her lack of dowry. They are equal, too, in sociability. Mr Knightley considers that being Emma's governess has given Mrs Weston an excellent training for marriage 'on the very matrimonial point of submitting your own will, and doing as you were bid'.

Equality is seen too in the Eltons' marriage; here, her accumulation of money carries his lack of funds. They develop a likeness in their speech and behaviour, Mr Elton becoming more vulgar, more self-important and more callous to the point where he cruelly snubs Harriet. (Emma doubts if he ever did behave like a gentleman.) He copies his wife's over-familiarity and name-dropping. Their snug contentment with each other provides an awful commentary on that romantic conclusion to almost every novel: the marriage.

Structure

Three structural patterns can be discerned in *Emma*, all working together to produce a complex awareness in the reader. These patterns are based on (a) character; (b) revelation; and (c) 'set pieces'. These patterns are not mechanical, nor regularly spaced within the book; they are interdependent, but each follows a logical sequence within itself.

Structure based on character

Much of the variety and delight of the novel comes with the introduction of new characters to this small area—and also their suspension or withdrawal from it—and the dominance of certain characters for the space of several chapters.

Introduction

In Chapters 1–15 we meet the Woodhouse family circle and the Highbury circle, concentric upon Emma: her father, Mr Knightley, the Westons (Chapters 1–2); the Bateses and Harriet (Chapter 3); Mr Elton Chapter 5); Isabella and Mr John Knightley (Chapters 11–13). These introductions build up a picture of life in Highbury, leading up to the big party scene at Randalls (Chapters 14–15) in which all are involved, even Harriet in her absence. After Mr Elton's declaration (Chapter 16), he is withdrawn (Chapter 17), and the next phase of character structure begins. Chapters 18–23 are much concerned with providing a 'build-up', a sense of anticipation, for the introduction of three new characters: Frank Churchill, Jane Fairfax, and Mrs Elton. Chapter 18 starts 'Mr Frank Churchill did not come', and he continues not to come until

Chapter 23. Jane Fairfax is only a suspicion in Emma's mind in Chapter 19, and even when we hear her history (Chapter 20) and she appears (Chapter 21) she does not emerge as a personality until much later in the novel. In Chapter 22 we hear about Mrs Elton, her background and fortune, but she does not appear in Highbury until Chapter 32. These anticipatory build-ups to the characters are very good preparation for their periods of dominance in the novel.

Domination

Frank Churchill dominates the novel from Chapters 24 to 31. He is a disrupting influence on Highbury, arriving and disappearing, starting plans for balls that have to be cancelled, but affecting everybody's life in some way or another. Mrs Elton is pre-eminent from Chapters 32 to 36. Whereas Frank Churchill imported an aura of metropolitan grandeur, Mrs Elton imports one of trade, cash and Bristol vulgarity, which she airs unmercifully at the many social gatherings she attends. Jane Fairfax, although present in Highbury from Chapter 20, does not become dominant until Chapter 41, when we and Emma become positively aware of her. Emma herself is always present in the foreground, as also is Mr Knightley, who is always nearby in the flesh or present in her thoughts.

Structure based on revelation and reflection

The structure based on the revelation of some truth to Emma, followed by a period of anguished reflection on her part, is one of the most marked and memorable features of the novel. There are five such revelations. First, Mr Elton's declaration to Emma in the carriage (Chapter 15), which, coming after her strenuous campaign to marry him to Harriet, brings 'pain and humiliation', mortification and shame, in a chapter entirely devoted to self-searching reflection (Chapter 16). The next revelation of her own insufficiency to Emma is provided by Mr Knightley, when he points out exactly what she has done in being rude to Miss Bates: it is not the heartless jest, but that someone in her position should make it to someone as poor and defenceless as Miss Bates (Chapter 43). Again, this truth brings humiliation to Emma; on understanding it she is 'agitated, mortified, grieved', and eventually feels 'the warmth of true contrition' (Chapters 43–4). The next truth to penetrate Emma's 'blindness' is a double revelation; that of the secret engagement of Frank Churchill and Jane Fairfax, immediately followed by the disclosure that Harriet is in love with Mr Knightley and thinks that he loves her (Chapter 46). This leads to two chapters of self-analysis and recrimination by Emma (Chapters 47–8), her realisation that she loves Mr Knightley, is dependent upon him, and has probably lost him through her stupidity. Following immediately upon this agonised reflection comes Mr Knightley's revelation that he loves Emma (Chapter 49)—a point at which many novels end. In *Emma*, however, we may expect a further period of reflection on the heroine's part. Emma is too happy for the agony of humiliation which she has experienced at other times, but she does undergo four chapters of acute worry 'and her mind had to pass again and again through every bitter reproach and sorrowful regret that had ever surrounded it' (Chapters 50–3). She cannot escape instantly the problems caused by her manipulation of others' emotions, and it is not until the final revelation, that Harriet is to marry Robert Martin (Chapter 54), that Emma can achieve 'the perfect happiness of the union' with Mr Knightley.

Structure based on 'set pieces'

Within the routine life of Hartfield and Highbury, so economically evoked throughout the novel, there are certain high points thrown into relief; often built up to,and often involving almost all our acquaintances. The characteristic 'set piece' is a party, at which the bringing together of the characters can establish a certain public position, or a new grouping be established. One of these is the Coles' party (Chapter 26) in which Frank Churchill is very openly attentive to Emma; in which she sides as it were with him against Jane Fairfax in discussing her suspicions about Mr Dixon; in which the piano affords a talking-point for everyone. Another set-piece is the dinner party which Emma gives for the Eltons (Chapters 34–5), in which Mrs Elton's officious meddling and lack of breeding and Jane Fairfax's firmness and dignity stand out; and in which the warm circle of 'concentrated objects' at Hartfield contrasts with outer darkness of governessing to which Jane Fairfax is soon to be consigned. The long awaited, long anticipated ball at the Crown Inn is another such set piece, narrated through the delighted exclamations of Miss Bates. Mr Elton proves himself no gentleman by humiliating Harriet; Mr Knightley proves he is one by rescuing her; Emma thinks that Frank Churchill admires her, but we see his attention to Jane Fairfax; and Emma and Mr Knightley dance. Two outdoor set pieces come close together: the strawberry picking at Donwell Abbey (Chapter 42) and the picnic to Box Hill (Chapter 43). The first is remarkable for its scenery and setting, and for the harmony of all except the tormented Jane Fairfax and Frank Churchill; the second for the disharmony of the whole party, for Emma's putting herself outside the polite society of Highbury for the moment by her flirting and rudeness, and worse, for her cutting herself off from Mr Knightley's regard.

There are two less crowded set pieces which are equally memorable in their settings, but are well prepared and dramatic. The first is Mr Elton's declaration of love to Emma in the carriage (Chapter 15), with the snow outside, the party left behind, the isolation, the pent-up emotion, the trapped feeling within the carriage. The other is another tête-à-tête: Mr Knightley's declaration to Emma in the shrubbery where 'the exquisite sight, smell, sensation of nature, tranquil, warm, and brilliant after a storm' surrounds the explaining lovers and both turn from distress to happiness (Chapter 49).

Plot

The 'outer' and 'inner' plots of *Emma* can be separated for the purposes of analysis. 'What is happening' and 'What Emma thinks is happening' diverge and converge at different points in the story. The reader's awareness of both these lines in the plot, his recognition that his own suspicions, and not Emma's fancy, were right, contribute to his enjoyment of the novel. In Chapters 1 to 15, Emma *thinks* that Mr Elton and Harriet are in love with each other. The reader gradually begins to suspect that 'what is happening' is that Mr Elton is interested in Emma. The 'revelation' of Mr Elton's proposal in the carriage (Chapter 16) resolves the differences: we were right, Emma was wrong, and she has to adjust to this new fact. From Chapter 18 to 30, Emma thinks that she and Frank Churchill are in love, and that Jane Fairfax is having an intrigue with Mr Dixon. On further consideration however, she decides that 'she could still do without Frank Churchill, and that he must learn to do without her'. So from Chapters 31 to 46 she is convinced that Harriet and Frank Churchill are interested in each other. Throughout both these sections, the reader is becoming more convinced of what is really happening. From hints and signals we grasp that there is a romantic connection between Frank Churchill and Jane Fairfax. In this, Chapter 41 is pivotal: here Mr Knightley observes and articulates the 'symptoms of attachment' between Frank Churchill and Jane Fairfax. Now Frank Churchill is in relationship with three women. On the surface he appears to be attached to Emma; in Emma's mind, he is attached to Harriet; in fact, and in Mr Knightley's suspicions, he is attached to Jane Fairfax. The revelation of Chapter 46 destroys Emma's theories about Frank Churchill and Harriet and about Jane Fairfax and Mr Dixon; she has quickly to readjust to the new fact of Frank Churchill and Jane Fairfax. Her adjustment is a painful one, however: from Harriet's reaction to the engagement she is led to believe that Harriet and Mr Knightley are in love. From Chapters 46 to 48 she suffers under this delusion, while the reader is gradually confirming his interpretation that Mr Knightley and Emma are meant for each other. After the proposal in the shrubbery, 'what is happening' and 'what Emma thinks is happening' are the same as regards the Eltons, Frank Churchill, Jane

Fairfax, Emma herself and Mr Knightley, and only Harriet's fate remains in doubt. With her engagement to Robert Martin, that eventuality against which Emma had set her face, but which we and Mr Knightley suspected to be the ideal match all along, the actual world and Emma's notion of it merge, and the inner and outer plots fuse.

Characterisation

The characterisation in *Emma* is masterly: the characters are so comic yet so convincing; so horrific yet so human. There are various ways of polarising the characters: they can be divided, for instance, into introverts and extroverts, or into those who do or do not develop; there are characters whose true nature is not revealed until we know the truth of the 'intrigue'.

Introverted and extroverted characters

'Society' is not just the background to *Emma*: it is the world order. The aim of an Austen character is to integrate well with society. The only 'morality' in the novel is concerned with how the characters treat other people, and Emma's progress in the novel is in large measure her adjustment to society.

Characters in the novel can be differentiated according to the degree of their integration into society. The introverted characters are those who look inward, into themselves, and are selfishly or thoughtlessly unaware of others; the extroverted characters are those who look outwards, at other people, away from themselves.

Mr John Knightley is an introvert who wishes only to stay within his own family, his 'concentrated objects' of affection. Mr Woodhouse is the epitome of introversion, although this is sometimes disguised as concern for others. He is primarily worried about his own health, his own comfort, his own undisturbed routine; his interest in Mr Knightley's shoes being specked with mud or Jane Fairfax's stockings damp is merely a reflection of this preoccupation. He must have a hot fire on a summer's day, and to justify it, may invite others to warm themselves by it; but his true concern is for himself. He cannot look outwards to his own daughter and see when she needs guidance, support, company or a husband. Jane Fairfax appears totally introverted—reserved, cold, neither making nor responding to any gesture of friendship. Even Mr Knightley dislikes her reserve, her lack of an 'open temper'. In her, until the engagement is made public, we see the forced and painful introversion of a mind 'pent up within itself'. Mrs Elton's pose is to be extroverted—to feign a great interest in others, to find a job for Jane Fairfax, to form a music society to occupy Emma. But in fact she is thinking of herself all the time; she does not actually listen when Jane Fairfax says she does not want the job. Mr Elton works very hard at being an extrovert and 'pleasing the ladies', but we sense no true interest in other people.

Isabella, although finely tuned to her family's happiness, looks out at others. Unlike her husband, she loves all her old acquaintances and visits with assiduity; unlike her sister, she praises Jane Fairfax and Miss Bates and takes the trouble to look at their good points. Mr Weston is an extroverted character, 'a disengaged and social man'. His great love of the social life does at one point lend some truth to John Knightley's accusations of insensitivity: during the dinner party he has known for some time that it was snowing, but has not told them so as 'not to disturb Mr Woodhouse', thus putting his joy in company above his guests' comfort. Miss Bates is an extrovert, totally concerned with others: never a mite of self-pity for her poverty; all praise and thanks, all interest, all delight in the happiness of others.

Harriet's tendency is to be extrovert—to look with wonder and admiration at Emma, at Robert Martin, at his family; to fit happily into their family, and into Hartfield. She can find things to admire in Mr Elton on demand. But Emma makes her think of herself, and finally, no longer self-effacing, she relates everything to herself: her self-centredness finds nothing 'so very wonderful' in the idea of Mr Knightley's marrying her.

Mr Knightley is genuinely interested in other people, from William Larkins to Mr Woodhouse. It is he who sends his carriage for Jane Fairfax and Miss Bates; who showers them with cooking apples; who advises Robert Martin; who bothers to get to know Harriet and revise his opinions of her.

Frank Churchill has all the social skills of his father, but is very self-seeking; in trying to juggle Mr Churchill's money and his engagement he is blind to the needs of his fiancée. While he appears to integrate himself into society, he is actually flouting its conventions.

Emma herself is not easy to categorise as introvert or extrovert. She is an intriguing balance of both. In her excellence as a housekeeper, her hostessly skill, her immediate interest in Harriet, we see evidence of concern for and engagement with other people. But like Mrs Elton she does not listen to what people say. And her all-consuming 'fancy' is an introverted quality. It blinds her to the true state of affairs, the true needs and feelings of others.

Introversion is not necessarily a harmful quality, when used correctly, and it is through Emma's powers of looking in at herself, through her capacity for self-analysis, that she finally finds herself and her true relation to society.

Static and dynamic characters

Another useful distinction between the characters in *Emma* is that of development. 'Static' characters remain unchanged in the course of the novel. 'Dynamic' characters develop. Mrs Elton, for example, flies fully fledged into Highbury. Her airs and graces, her Maple Grove, her desire to be 'first', her pushing ways and her vulgarity are all there from the beginning, and each new horror simply confirms our first opinion of her vulgarity. Miss Bates does not change; she is unfailingly worthy and unfailingly wordy throughout. Her way of taking Emma's hurtful remark at Box Hill is generous, as we should expect. Mr Woodhouse is another entirely predictable character, whose comic effect on the novel is mainly due to this predictability—the words doctor, sea air, carriage and marriage are all guranteed to start him off on a well-worn conversational track. Isabella and Mr John Knightley also remain static throughout the novel; he is observant of Mr Elton's interest in Emma at the beginning, and of his brother's in the end; he has an abiding distaste for parties and visits. Again this predictability makes us laugh. With the exception of the constantly faithful and ill-treated Robert Martin, and Isabella, the unfailingly worthy wife, mother, daughter and friend, it can be seen that the static characters are the ones who provide the comedy in *Emma*.

The dynamic characters, those who change or develop, who are too complex for pure comedy, are Harriet Smith, Jane Fairfax, Mr Knightley and Emma herself. Harriet, in particular, develops—and not at all for the better. When we first meet her, she is a 'humble, grateful little girl'. She is unassuming, 'blaming nobody' for her disappointment because 'the affection of such a man as Mr Elton would have been too great ... she never could have deserved him'. How different her later character, presumptuous enough to aspire to Mr Knightley. At the last, Emma even finds 'some hint of resentment' in Harriet's hardened heart.

Jane Fairfax's development is stunted by Frank Churchill's insistence on a secret engagement, and it is only at the end that we see this restrained, reserved woman in her 'cloak of politeness' develop and blossom as she ought to have been able to do since her stay at Weymouth. She can smile, speak and respond; she even changes physically: 'There was consciousness, animation, and warmth; there was every thing which her countenance or manner could ever have wanted'; she has 'a blush and an hesitation which Emma thought infinitely more becoming to her than all the elegance of all her usual composure'. She develops to the point of being able to chide Frank Churchill, and Mr Knightley sees that she will have the strength of mind to improve him.

Mr Knightley's character is apparently static; he is a pillar of strength, a tower of wisdom, a fount of good advice and rationality. But his character undergoes a sudden dynamic change under the charge of a new emotion less noble than he has previously felt: that of jealousy. He explains that his jealousy of Frank Churchill has precipitated his rush to London 'to learn to be indifferent'. He develops into someone who can only propose hesitantly ('Have I no chance of ever succeeding?'); someone who suddenly 'cannot make speeches'; someone unsure and unselfconfident. His jealousy releases his dictatorial spirit into love ('He had been in love with Emma, and jealous of Frank Churchill, from about the same period, one sentiment having probably enlightened him as to the other').

Emma's character changes for the better, as we have seen: her progression towards self-knowledge is faithfully charted; she who was vain, superior and thoughtless at the beginning of the novel becomes humble, reflective and fulfilled at its end.

Concealed characters

When Frank Churchill and Jane Fairfax were first seen after their engagement was made public, 'a glimpse was caught through the blind, of two figures passing near the window'. This glimpse is indicative of the half-vision in which we see both of them through the novel. They are 'concealed' characters. While the intrigue or deception goes on, we cannot know them, and have to take them at their face value: Frank Churchill seems devoted to Emma, rude about Jane Fairfax and vain about having his hair cut. Jane Fairfax seems impossibly reserved, quiet and negative. We cannot assess their characters until we have the key to the intrigue, when Jane Fairfax's cold silence can be seen as stoic heroism—what courage it must have taken to play the piano and sing while her fiancé flirted with Emma! Frank Churchill can be seen as more devious and less frivolous than we had thought. He has been more dishonourable to Emma than had appeared; his flirtation with her at Box Hill was neither sincere nor due to high spirits, but was a cruel attack on Jane Fairfax, with whom he had quarrelled. He had written his 'handsome letter' from Weymouth instead of attending his father's wedding not through lack of filial duty nor through spinelessness in the face of Mrs Churchill, but because he was busy getting engaged to Jane Fairfax.

The engagement at Weymouth is one of several interesting concealed passages in the novel. How did two such disparate characters fall in love? What did they say at the Bateses over the spectacles? How did they quarrel on the road between Donwell and Highbury? We might also wonder how the courtship between Mr Elton and Mrs Elton (then Miss Hawkins) went. His character could be called concealed in a way; his vulgarity is not visible until after his marriage.

The characters

Emma

One of the features of Jane Austen's characterisation is its precision. Often, as soon as a character is introduced, we are given a summing-up of his or her character, which may later be developed or modified but which will be consistent with his or her behaviour throughout the novel. Thus, Emma is described in the very first sentence as 'handsome, clever, and rich, with a comfortable home and happy disposition', and by the fourth paragraph we have been told of the 'real evils' of her situation and character that will provide most of the drama in the novel: 'the power of having rather too much her own way, and a disposition to think a little too well of herself'.

Jane Austen thought that nobody but herself would like Emma very much because she was so imperfect a heroine—but just as Mr Knightley finally declares her 'faultless in spite of her faults', we are won over by her, however infuriated we may be by her blindness, her stubbornness and her unjustified selfconfidence.

Physically, she is 'the complete picture of grown-up health'. We admire her physical stamina as she runs her house efficiently, arranges her entertainments, cossets her father, plays with her nieces and nephews. But her mental vigour is dangerous. Once she has had an idea she pursues it relentlessly: no sooner is Harriet introduced to Hartfield than she is there day and night; no sooner is she aimed at Mr Elton than Emma makes sure that he is there almost as constantly. Many of Emma's failings are the obverse side of her good points: that quality so excellent in a hostess, a spirit 'never indifferent to the credit of doing every thing well and attentively, with the real good-will of a mind delighted with its own ideas' is akin to the destructive single-mindedness with which she manipulates Harriet.

Emma is 'never loth to be first'. She wants to be first at the ball, likes being first with her father, and cannot bear the thought of yielding first place with Mr Knightley to anyone else. It is he who tells us most of Emma's shortcomings: 'Emma has been meaning to read more every since she was twelve years old . . .'. She will never submit to any thing requiring industry and patience, and a subjection of the fancy to the understanding'. His prophetic dictum 'I would like to see Emma in love, and in some doubt of a return' pierces to the root of Emma's failings: it is her inexperience of love that makes her so sure that it can be 'organised', so well able to switch it on and off towards Frank Churchill, so insensitive about its effects on other people.

Mr Knightley's misgivings about Emma's fancy are well founded. She is proud of being an 'imaginist', and sees her fancy as 'penetration'.

Frank Churchill is 'the young man, of which her imagination had already given her such instinctive knowledge' before they met. She *likes* fantasising: when she first weaves a story around Jane Fairfax, to relieve a boring conversation with Miss Bates, she welcomes it as 'an ingenious and animating suspicion'. At the Coles', 'that very dear part of Emma, her fancy, received an amusing supply'; it makes her come to conclusions about people ('the highly probable circumstances of an attachment to Mr Dixon') without ever actually thinking about them. She neither feels anything for people, nor recognises that they have feelings. And when she imagines a romance for herself with Frank Churchill, she never sees herself as emotionally affected: 'the conclusion of every imaginary declaration on his side was that she *refused him*'. This impersonal vision of other people is the cause of most of Emma's misdeeds. It is Mr Knightley who helps to feel for people, imploring her 'compassion' for Miss Bates, making her 'heart' grow 'kinder towards Jane'. And when 'it darted through her, with the speed of an arrow, that Mr Knightley must marry no one but herself', it makes her resolve 'to understand, thoroughly understand her own heart'. In loving her, and in inspiring love in her, Mr Knightley makes Emma feel at last: it is the triumph of heart over head.

Jane Fairfax

Jane Fairfax is the model of 'accomplishment': her playing and singing eclipse Emma's, she is beautiful and elegant. The impression she makes on us is of icy reserve; her 'cloak of politeness' makes her almost invisible. The contrast with Emma is everywhere drawn to our notice, and like so many of the women in the novel, affects our view of her. Their circumstances too are in opposition: Emma is rich, has her own establishment and need not work; Jane Fairfax is poor, has to earn her living, and will have to live in others' houses. Jane Fairfax is a negative image of Emma, cold, ghostly and sickly, where Emma is warm, lively and healthy. Where Emma is active and initiating, Jane Fairfax is passive to the point of paralysis: her only positive action is in rebuffing Emma when at last she tries to make friends. Her secret engagement accounts for much of this frigidity: she cannot be at ease in company until it is revealed, and only then can she relax into friendliness. 'Emma had never seen her look so well, so lovely, so engaging. There was consciousness, animation and warmth; there was every thing which her countenance or manner could ever have wanted'. She knows she has been ' "so cold and artificial—I had always a part to act" '. We admire, with Frank Churchill, that 'resolution of character' which has carried her through her time of strain.

Harriet Smith

Harriet Smith is to a certain extent a cipher. She is very visible to us, her beauty and her silliness equally striking; but her natural tendency is to be malleable, and only someone with an unformed character would allow Emma to 'stage-manage' her as she does. We have seen the progression of this 'humble, grateful little girl' to hardness under Emma's rule; and Mr Knightley sees that the danger to Emma's character from Harriet is just as great. She will bring out the worst in Emma because 'her ignorance is hourly flattery'. Although Harriet is almost always of the party, she hardly ever speakes in public; her most noteworthy utterances are to Emma alone or with Mr Elton; her ludicrous mementoes of him show up her pathetic silliness. Her apparent ability to fall in love with one man after another is not necessarily part of her nature; she did attempt to cling to Robert Martin despite Emma's persuasion. Mr Knightley sees that her circumstances are unenviable, 'the natural daughter of nobody knows whom, with no respectable relations or connections, and no money'. His recognition of her as an 'amiable, artless girl' who is 'more conversable than I expected' suggests that those feminine, cheerful ways almost eclipsed by Emma are still with her, and that she deserves Robert Martin's fidelity.

Isabella

'Isabella was too much like Emma' says Mr Knightley, having tried to blot out his jealousy by visiting the John Knightleys in London. And they are alike in their domestic capabilities and family affection, particularly their consideration of their father. But they are different enough for us to question certain points in Emma's character. Isabella is supposed to be less intelligent—but she generously sees Jane Fairfax's good qualities and recommends her as a friend to Emma. Isabella is the 'worshipping wife' who 'cannot bear to stay behind her husband' and who has a 'Very true, my love' for his every remark. Emma, who declares that she will not marry, seems self-sufficient by comparison; but Isabella's standards are in fact those that Emma comes to eventually when she falls in love. Isabella likes to be sociable; she is much more tolerant than Emma, having the 'habit of love for old acquaintance'; she would never have snubbed Miss Bates. Isabella's greatest contribution to the novel is through the comedy in her exchanges with her father.

Mrs Weston

Mrs Weston is another of the very feminine characters set against Emma's limited femininity. She has loved and looked after Emma for eight years, and now looks after her husband and finally her new baby. She is warm, agreeable and sparkling, as we see from her conversation with Mr Knightley about Emma. She echoes, or has perhaps encouraged, Emma's fancy: before she herself has even met Frank Churchill, she has planned a marriage between them; she is just as quick as Emma to hazard guesses about Jane Fairfax's pianoforte, devoting some ingenuity to her theory that Mr Knightley had sent it, and planning a marriage between them with romantic enthusiasm.

Miss Bates

Miss Bates is a marvellous mixture of the admirable and the unbearable: we know she is kind, cheerful, noble in the face of fearful odds, but we can sympathise with Emma's dread of her flow of words. Miss Bates is quite the opposite of any romantic idea of what a woman should be: she is 'neither young, handsome, rich, nor married'. She has no money, and has had no life; 'her youth was passed without distinction, and her middle of life was devoted to the care of a failing mother'. What we are told about her on her first introduction, and what shines clearly through all her comic appearances in the book, is that she has the gift of happiness, of universal good-will given and received. Miss Bates's unfinished sentences tell us more of life in Highbury than anything else in the novel; her ramblings are inexplicably graphic and extraordinarily funny: 'I do congratulate you, Mrs Weston, most warmly. He seems every thing the fondest parent could . . .'. Her reaction to Emma's taunt about her dullness is humble and shows up Emma's callowness: 'Ah!—well—to be sure. Yes, I see what she means (turning to Mr Knightley), and I will try to hold my tongue. I must make myself very disagreeable, or she would not have said such a thing to an old friend'. As usual, it is Mr Knightley who pins down the situation: 'Were she a woman of fortune, I would have every harmless absurdity to take its chance': Miss Bates's poverty that excuses, even ennobles, her ridiculousness.

Mr Knightley

Mr Knightley's outstanding gift is his perception. It will be noticed how often in these notes the phrase 'as Mr Knightley sees' or 'as Mr Knightley says' occurs. He can see through everybody—not only their bad points, but their good ones. He is flexible enough to see Harriet's better qualities, having been the first to warn Emma of her drawbacks as a companion. He is a shrewd judge of motive and behaviour; he tells Emma well in advance that 'Mr Elton may speak sentimentally but he will act rationally', and is the first to suspect Frank Churchill 'of some inclination to trifle with Jane Fairfax'. It is Emma who suffers—and profits—most from his clear vision. Their long acquaintance allows him to accuse her at various times of being indolent at her piano, unkind to Jane Fairfax, unladylike in her 'insolence' to Miss Bates. In his constant chiding, he is of course being much kinder to her than her fond, indulgent, father, sister and ex-governess, whose refusal to see any fault in her has largely led to her vanity. Mr Knightley's uprightness in all moral and social matters is taken for granted all through the novel, by the other characters and by the narrator; but it is Emma who uses him most as the model of all that is correct. She thinks his manner, appearance and actions flawless. His magnificent and orderly estate is a symbol of all that she deems finest in the English gentleman. Yet for all his perfection, he is human and likeable: he can laugh at himself as well as at her; he is kind enough to save Harriet from social distress by dancing with her; and the combination of jealousy and indignation that he admits towards Frank Churchill shows him to be far from the remote paragon of all the virtues we first think him: 'The feeling of the warmest friendship—Indignation—Abominable scoundrel!'

Mr Woodhouse

Emma's father apparently has two different dominating characteristics, but we have seen that his selfishness is the true motive for his consideration for other people. His attitude to Emma shows a similar apparent kindness; but in being too indulgent with her, in praising her indiscriminately, he is relinquishing a father's duty. His great concern for her blinds her, and everybody else, to the fact that while she gives him all possible care, attention and comfort, he gives her nothing but the assurance of riches. His sociability is limited to those who will entertain or be entertained exclusively on his terms: 'his horror of late hours and large dinner parties made him unfit for any acquaintance, but such as would visit him on his own terms'. The comedy that is always attached to Mr Woodhouse comes from his concentration on himself, his extreme hypochondria, and his intense preoccupation with externals (Mr Knightley's dusty shoes, Jane Fairfax's damp stockings) encapsulated in view of the portrait of Harriet: 'So prettily done! Just as your drawings always are, my dear. I do not know any body who draws as well as you do. The only thing I do not throughly like is, that she seems to be sitting out of doors, with only a little shawl over her shoulders—and it makes one think she must catch cold.'

Mr John Knightley

Mr John Knightley is the same sort of bluff Englishman as his brother George; they greet each other undemonstratively. He has an acute sense of family, is irritable but soothable. Like Mr Woodhouse, he hates visiting, dinner parties and most social events. He has cooler manners than his brother, and is less communicative, but like him is a shrewd and observant judge of character and action—it is he who warns Emma not to be too familiar with Mr Elton. Like his brother, he represents a whole class to Emma: she reflects at Donwell Abbey upon all that the Woodhouses have gained by Isabella's marrying him and associating them with 'a family of such true gentility, untainted in blood and understanding.—Some faults of temper John Knightley had; but Isabella had connected herself unexceptionably'.

Mr Elton

Mr Elton, we may forget, is a handsome young man—'a very pretty young man', 'a man of six or seven-and-twenty'. He acts in a crabbed, elderly way with his dreadful gallantries to Emma and Harriet, his pomposity and 'parade'. Emma moves from recommending him to Harriet as a 'gentleman' to finding he lacks elegance; he talks nonsense long before she is disgusted by his advances to her in the carriage. He has many of the qualities of Mrs Elton long before he meets and marries her: he pushes himself forwards, talks inflatedly, assumes familiarity in an unwelcome fashion—'How well they suit one another', says Frank Churchill. Both are rude and vindictive, as Mr Knightley observes when he crudely spurns Harriet at the ball: 'He was warm in his reprobation of Mr Elton's conduct; it had been unpardonable rudeness; and Mrs Elton's looks also receive the due share of censure. "They aimed at wounding more than Harriet," said he. Emma, why is it that they are your enemies?' At least, when he snubs Harriet, Emma loses her idea that he was ever the gentleman she had fancied him: 'This was Mr Elton! the amiable, obliging, gentle Mr Elton!'; the unpleasantness of the couple is confirmed as 'smiles of high glee passed between him and his wife.'

Frank Churchill

The character of Frank Churchill is, as we have seen, not possible to assess until one knows his secret. Our impression of his deviousness, materialism and lack of consideration are not wiped out by the letter in which he tries to excuse himself: it is, if anything, heightened. But for all that, he is an attractive character, breezing into provincial Highbury with news of a wider world—even threatening to go abroad! His jokes, even his double joke upon Emma, are engaging; his flattery is performed with style. Emma sees that they have many qualities in common, especially the ability to laugh at themselves ('Oh! no—what an impudent dog I was!—How could I dare—'). They both laugh heartily at other people, too, as she says: 'I am sure it was a source of high entertainment to you, to feel that you were taking us all in.—Perhaps I am the readier to suspect, because, to tell you the truth, I think it might have been some amusement to myself in the same situation. I think there is a little likeness between us.'

Mr Weston

Mr Weston is at the opposite pole from Mr John Knightley, who assesses him thus: 'Mr Weston is rather an easy, cheerful tempered man, than a man of strong feelings; he takes things as he finds them, and makes enjoyment of them somehow or other, depending, I suspect, much more upon what is called *society* for his comforts, that is, upon the power of eating and drinking, and playing whist with his neighbours five times a-week, than upon family affection, or any thing that home affords'. Mr Knightley despises such sociability; Isabella finds it shocking that he should have parted with his son (though that was not an unusual occurrence at the time); but she does reflect that he flew her son's kite for him very agreeably. In the novel, Mr Weston represents the extreme of the extrovert, of the amiable character and of the social animal.

Style

Narrative

The narrator of *Emma* establishes from the beginning an analytic and slightly moralising tone: 'The real evils indeed of Emma's situation were the power of having rather too much her own way, and a disposition to think too well of herself'. The narrator is omniscient, knowing everything about the characters' inmost thoughts as well as their actions. On the whole the narrator uses this power of inward looking to tell us about what is going on in Emma's mind: we also enter other characters' minds from time to time (Mrs Weston's thoughts on leaving the Woodhouses in Chapter 2, or Mr Knightley's first suspicions of Frank Churchill and Jane Fairfax in Chapter 41).

The narrative is orderly in content and style. The Woodhouses' friends are set out in two groups, inner and outer, clearly 'labelled' for us (Chapter 3). And as the lay-out is orderly, so is the expression of it: Mr Weston 'had made his fortune, bought his house and obtained his wife', an orderly sequence, like the description of Mr Woodhouse: 'from his long residence at Hartfield, and his good nature, from his fortune, his house and his daughter, he could command the visits of his own little circle'. (Here the sequence is not a mere list; its five components are differently grouped by their prepositions). Similarly when Harriet hears of Mr Elton's engagement, 'before their first conversation was over, she had talked herself into all the sensations of curiosity, wonder and regret, pain and pleasure' as to Miss Hawkins. Another consistent feature of the narrative is a balanced construction. This can be very simple: when she met Harriet, 'Emma was as much pleased with her manners as her person,' or more complex, as when Mr Knightley considers the ball: 'Either because he did not dance himself, or because the plan had been formed without his being consulted, he seemed resolved that it should not interest him, determined against its exciting any present curiosity, or affording him any future amusement'. Balanced antitheses illustrate the 'sad warfare' of Mr Woodhouse's feelings: 'He loved to have the cloth laid, because it had been the fashion of his youth; but his conviction of suppers being very unwholesome made him rather sorry to see anything put on it; and while his hospitality would have welcomed his visitors to every thing, his care for their health made him grieve that they would eat'.

The smoothness and balance of the narrative is broken for specific moments of high tension, one of the most effective being the description of Mr Elton's advances to Emma in the carriage (Chapter 15). This is particularly comic because the passage starts with Emma resolutely trying to speak with 'exquisite calmness', a composure which is quickly lost in a flurry of dashes that lasts for four pages: 'To restrain him as much as might be, by her own manners, she was immediately preparing to speak with exquisite calmness and gravity of the weather and the night; but scarcely had she begun, scarcely had they passed the sweep-gate and joined the other carriage, than she found her subject cut up—her hand seized—her attention demanded, and Mr Elton actually making violent love to her ... hoping—fearing—adoring—ready to die if she refused him... 'It really was so. Without scruple—without apology—without much apparent diffidence...'. (This break-up in syntax is echoed in the characters' speech, here and at other times of stress; it also occurs in their thought-patterns). We see a similar dislocation of narrative smoothness when Emma has to tell Harriet that Mr Elton is not interested in her: 'She had to destroy all the hopes which she had been so industriously feeding—to appear in the ungracious character of the one preferred—and acknowledge herself grossly mistaken'.

The narrative is also remarkable for the occasional flashing phrase: of Emma and Mr Elton, 'their straightforward emotions left no room for the little zigzags of embarrassment'; of Frank Churchill's letter, the rare simple expression 'unadorned as it was by any such broad wreath of gallantry'. The narrative can also make small graduations and distinctions—Mr Robert Martin meets Emma with Harriet, and 'after looking very respectfully at her, looked with most unfeigned satisfaction at her companion'. This delicacy of touch is apparent when Emma and Frank Churchill meet after both engagements have been announced: 'they met readily and smiling, but with a consciousness which at first allowed little to be said' (Chapter 54), or when Mr Knightley reads Frank Churchill's explanatory letter in Emma's company: 'and, excepting one momentary glance at her, instantly withdrawn, in the fear of giving pain—no remembrance of Box Hill seemed to exist'. Oblique and tactful narrative veils Mr Knightley's proposal when she becomes 'his own, by hand and word'.

Dialogue

Emma is extremely critical about how people use language, as we see from her reaction to Robert Martin's letter to Harriet: 'As a composition it would not have disgraced a gentleman; the language, though plain, was strong and unaffected'. The language and form of conversation matters equally; the narrator often guides us: 'Mr Knightley, who had nothing of ceremony about him, was offering by his short, decided answers, an amusing contrast to the protracted apologies and civil hesitations of the other' (Mr Woodhouse). The finer distinctions of conversation are seen by Mr Knightley himself: 'Mrs Elton does not talk *to* Miss Fairfax as she speaks *of* her'.

Dialogue is used by Jane Austen as an economical way of conveying peoples' own characters: Mr Woodhouse's fractiousness is demonstrated when he complains in the same breath about Randalls being 'so far' and 'such a little way'. Mrs Elton gives herself away the moment she opens her mouth, with her endless name-dropping, her mad aphorisms ('I always say this is quite one of the evils of matrimony'), her clichés ('Surrey is the garden of England') and her repetitions (the barouche-landau, Maple Grove and her 'inner resources' figuring large). Her vulgarity is revealed in the ways she talks about her husband alone—'my *caro sposo*', 'my lord and master', 'Mr E'. Emma's 'general rules' and her silly aphorisms about marriage show her as inexperienced; her brashness, lack of judgement and condescension are all revealed in her scornful dismissal of Robert Martin.

Characters and facts are also illustrated through the conversation of others. In talking playfully to Mr Knightley, Emma gives us a full account of Mr Weston and his way of life: 'Everybody said that Mr Weston would never marry again. Oh dear, no! Mr Weston, who had been a widower so long, and who seemed so perfectly comfortable without a wife, so constantly occupied either in his business in town or among his friends here, always acceptable wherever he went, always cheerful—Mr Weston need not spend a single evening in the year alone if he did not like it.' Many inflections, suggestions and details are conveyed in conversation. Chapter 5, for example, is entirely in dialogue except for the last paragraph. As Mrs Weston and Mr Knightley discuss Emma, we get a vivid sense of her physical appearance, which is never described by the narrator: 'Such an eye—the true hazle eye—and so brilliant! regular feature, open countenance, with a complexion! . . . There is health, not merely in her bloom, but in her air, her head, her glance'. We get an inkling of Mr Knightley's feelings for Emma too—'"I love to look at her"'.

While the dialogue of *Emma* is lively and spontaneous, much of it is formal, as was natural for the gentility of the time; it gives a balanced and well-organised impression, falling into antitheses, parallels and sequences. Emma's exhortation to Harriet to pull herself together is rhetorical as well as bracing, culminating in six progressive points: 'I have not said, exert yourself Harriet for my sake; think less, talk less of Mr Elton for my sake; because for your own sake rather, I would wish it to be done for the sake of what is more important than my comfort, a habit of self-command in you, a consideration of what is your duty, an attention to propriety, an endeavour to avoid the suspicions of others, to save your health and credit, and restore your tranquillity'. Because most of the dialogue is organised and sequential, it is particularly noticeable and effective when at moments of extreme stress, its syntax becomes disorganised. The articulate Mr Knightley becomes inarticulate when he commiserates with Emma before proposing; she, after a 'flutter of pleasure', replies 'You are very kind—but you are mistaken—and I must set you right.—I am not in want of that sort of compassion'.

Different styles and paces of conversation afford different experiences for the reader. Jane Fairfax's conversation is terse, Mrs Elton's headlong, Miss Bates's uncontrollable—her interminable panegyrics are funny to a degree. Mr Woodhouse's monologues too are highly comic, for example, that at the end of Chapter 3 in which he invites his guests to avoid practically all the food provided for them. Much of the comedy of the novel comes through the dialogue—Harriet speculating about Mr Elton's charade: 'Can it be Neptune? or a mermaid? or a shark?'; Mr Knightley shouting a well-overheard exchange with Miss Bates from the street below (Chapter 28); Isabella and Mr Woodhouse swapping the opinions of their doctors (Chapter 12). We laugh at Emma describing her own drawings: 'The corner of the sofa is very good', and at Mr Elton with his 'Exactly so', and his 'What a precious deposit' as he receives the portrait with a tender sigh.

Conversation is used too to convey the minutiae of life: the buzz of preparations for the ball—'You and Miss Smith, and Miss Fairfax, will be three, and the two Miss Coxes' repeated many times. Perhaps the triumph of direct speech in *Emma* is the description of the ball almost exclusively through the very long monologue of Miss Bates (Chapter 38), in her unmistakable voice: 'As the door opened she was heard, "So very obliging of you!—No rain at all. Nothing to signify. I do not care for myself. Quite thick shoes. And Jane declares—Well!—(as soon as she was within the door) Well! This is brilliant indeed!—This is admirable.—Excellently contrived, upon my word. Nothing wanting. Could not have imagined it.—So well lighted up.—Jane, Jane look—did you ever see any thing? Oh! Mr Weston, you must really have had Aladdin's lamp..."' and so on through shawls, hair, company, dresses and food.

Indirect speech

One of the most distinctive methods of description in *Emma* is close to the style of Miss Bates's view of the ball, but uses indirect speech with the intonation of real conversation. This can convey a sustained picture, as when Harriet describes at length her stay with the Martins (Chapter 4) or her brief visit to them (Chapter 23) It can replay what happened, and the indirect speaker's state of mind: Harriet describes meeting the Martins in Ford's shop: 'She had set out from Mrs Goddard's half an hour ago—she had been afraid it would rain ... who should come in, but Elizabeth Martin and her brother....' The indirect narrative drifts now and then into direct speech: 'Dear Miss Woodhouse! Only think. I thought I should have fainted ... Oh!'

Jane Fairfax describes (or fails to describe) Frank Churchill to Emma in this kind of indirect narrative (Chapter 20). The most splendid example of indirect narrative is, however, Mrs Elton's conversation during the strawberry party at Donwell Abbey, proceeding from pleasure to exhaustion in snatches: 'The best fruit in England—every body's favourite—always wholesome.—These the finest beds and the finest sorts.—Delightful to gather for one's self ... price of strawberries in London—abundance about Bristol—Maple Grove—cultivation—beds when to be renewed ... only objection to gathering strawberries the stooping—glaring sun—tired to death—could bear it no longer—must go and sit in the shade.'

Thought

The narrative is finely tuned to the characters' thoughts, closely following their progression. Emma has two 'distinct and independent' sentiments about her two friends: 'Mrs Weston was the object of a regard, which had its basis in gratitude and esteem. Harriet would be loved as one to whom she could be useful. For Mrs Weston there was nothing to be done; for Harriet every thing' (Chapter 4). Here the balanced sentences are not for stylistic purposes only; they help the fine analysis of abstract thought. Inmost reflections are often as orderly as formal conversation: 'a more serious, more dispiriting cogitation on what had been, and might be, and must be', or Emma finding Mrs Elton 'self-important, presuming, familiar, ignorant, and ill-bred'. There are brief mental notes ('Encouragement should be given') and trains of thought 'of a sort to run into great length'.

One of the most striking thought-processes is Emma's habit of addressing people in her head: she 'thinks to' Mr Elton: 'You know nothing of drawing. Don't pretend to be in raptures about mine' or 'Very well, Mr Elton, very well indeed. I have read worse charades.... This is saying very plainly—"pray, Miss Smith, give me leave to pay my addresses to you".... Humph—Harriet's ready wit!...' (Chapter 9)

Here we are privileged to 'see' Emma's thoughts—but we suspect, as she does not, that they are ill-founded: Mr Elton is thinking of Emma's own ready wit. We frequently feel this separation from Emma's thoughts when we know her fancy is running away with her: when she 'feels herself so well acquainted with' Frank Churchill, or thinks he wants 'to settle early in life' in a small house—'Enscombe could not make him happy', or when his 'unfortunate fancy for having his hair cut' preys on her thoughts until she comically (to us) 'thus moralised to herself ... "Wickedness is always wickedness but folly is not always folly".'

We feel no ironic separation from Emma's thoughts, however, in those great passages of self-analysis which come after each of her mistakes or humiliations—particularly Chapter 16, when she reflects on her misjudgement of Mr Elton, and Chapters 47 and 48 when she feels first guilt for having encouraged Harriet Smith to love Frank Churchill, then horror that she loves Mr Knightley, then alarm that she herself loves him. We see her anguish, her self-reproach, her mortification. We watch her wrestle with her emotions, examine her own motives, push herself painfully towards self-knowledge. These long, minute analyses of Emma's thoughts are very close to the modern technique of 'stream of consciousness' or 'interior monologue', the attempt to reproduce the spontaneous flow of thought which one finds in the work of Virginia Woolf (1882–1941) or James Joyce (1882–1941). The drama of the novel is the interior drama of Emma's mind: at the point of Mr Knightley's proposal (Chapter 49) the narrator justifies the novel's concentration on the swift inner movement of thought: 'While he spoke, Emma's mind was most busy, and with all the wonderful velocity of thought, had been able—and yet without losing a word—to catch and comprehend the exact truth of the whole'.

Background

Although the domestic background of *Emma* is neither catalogued nor insisted on, it is very clearly discernible: a well-run household; food from asparagus to egg-custard, from loins of pork to gruel; Pembroke tables, large circular tables, card-tables. All appear where necessary to reinforce the solid, three-dimensional world in which the characters live.

There is also an extremely powerful use of houses and scenery to symbolise or represent certain less tangible matters. The most notable descriptions of scenery occur during the visit to Donwell Abbey (Chapter 42). Here we see Mr Knightley's house and estate laid out before us in views and vistas—avenues of limes, banks, woods, farms, meadows, rivers, walls, pillars, ponds. The harmony of this scene strikes us; and we also learn that it means more to Emma than 'local colour': 'It was a sweet view—sweet to the eye and the mind. English verdure, English culture, English comfort, seen under a sun bright, without being oppressive'. It also represents a social order: the house 'was just what it ought to be, and it looked what it was—and Emma felt an increasing respect for it, as the residence of a family of such true gentility, untainted in blood and understanding'. She reflects that 'Isabella had connected herself unexceptionally', but we feel that the house represents Mr Knightley himself, and that her admiration is ultimately directed at him.

How different is the scene on the following day at Box Hill. Here all is disharmony. The scenery is not described in minute detail as at Donwell. One reason for this is that Donwell was fictitious and therefore not known to the reader, whereas Box Hill was a well-known and much-pictured beauty spot. Further, whereas Emma had a vivid conscious and subconscious awareness of Donwell, at Box Hill the scenery is almost unseen, obscured by Frank Churchill's 'flattery and merriment' as his spirits rise 'to a pitch almost unpleasant'. Emma wishes she could be alone and 'in tranquil observation of the beautiful views beneath her'.

At Donwell the sun had been 'bright, without being oppressive'. But even there Frank Churchill arrived, complaining of 'intolerable', 'excessive' heat. Tension accentuated by the weather is remarkable at several points in the novel. The snow which traps Emma with Mr Elton in the carriage heightens its claustrophobia. When Emma thinks that Mr Knightley is lost to her for ever, the weather echoes her misery and her bleak prospects: 'The evening of this day was very long, and melancholy, at Hartfield. The weather added what it could of gloom. A cold stormy rain set in, and nothing of July appeared but in the trees and shrubs, which the wind was despoiling, and the length of the day, which only made such cruel sights the longer visible'. Next day, the arrival of Mr Knightley and the joy of his proposal are prefigured by a change in the weather: 'in the afternoon it cleared; the wind changed into a softer quarter; the clouds were carried off; the sun appeared; it was summer again.... Never had the exquisite sight, smell, sensation of nature, tranquil, warm and brilliant after a storm, been more attractive to her'.

Irony

Irony of situation

Irony can take the form of a situation where what is happening means one thing to the person concerned, but something else to those who know what is going on. It involves the idea of an outer meaning for the person concerned, and an inner meaning for a privileged observer. The double irony of *Emma* is that whereas Emma thinks she is the privileged observer who knows what is going on, she is actually the dupe (as when we realise that Mr Elton is interested in her and not, as she thinks, in Harriet). And because she is duped not by the malevolence of anybody else, but purely through her own machinations, we cannot pity her excessively. Even Frank Churchill, who uses her, is offered the opportunity to do so by her own premature assumption that they are good friends, and by her indiscretions about Jane Fairfax.

Many of Emma's own pronouncements underline this double irony: her 'I thought I could not be so deceived' is about as sensible as Harriet's 'Whatever you say is always right'. The perfect expression of it is found when Mr John Knightley warns her that she is encouraging Mr Elton. She blisteringly, and as it turns out, quite wrongly, announces '"Mr Elton and I are very good friends, and nothing more;" and she walked on, amusing herself in the consideration of the blunders which often arise from a partial knowledge of circumstance' (Chapter 13). There is also a happier kind of irony of situation: Mr Knightley, jealous of Frank Churchill, not knowing that Emma loves him; Emma, jealous of Harriet Smith, not knowing that Mr Knightley loves her.

As well as this irony (in which Emma cannot see the signs that we can see so clearly) there is a retrospective irony, in which we can look back and see what was happening. When Emma thinks Frank Churchill is about to declare his love for her, we know that she has misinterpreted something, but we do not know until we read his letter that he was about to tell her of his engagement to Jane Fairfax. We do not realise how very misguided she was until we know of the engagement and we look back at her discussing Jane Fairfax's eccentric hairstyle and pale face, or surmising about the boat disaster and the dashing Mr Dixon: 'If I had been there I think I would have made some discoveries'.

Irony of tone

The narrator's dry tone gives an ironic flavour: 'Frank Churchill was one of the boasts of Highbury, and a lively curiosity to see him prevailed, though the compliment was so little returned that he had never been there in his life'; 'Mr Weston, who had called in for half a minute, in order to hear that his son was handsome'. Mr Woodhouse is often treated in this way: after Mrs Weston's wedding, he 'was no longer teased by being wished joy of so sorrowful an event; and the wedding-cake, which had been a great distress to him, was all eat up'. A typically laconic comment contrasts Miss Bates's enthusiasm with Jane Fairfax's lack of it: '"Jane, you have never seen Mr Elton!—no wonder that you have such a curiosity to see him". Jane's curiosity did not appear of that absorbing nature as wholly to occupy her.' Much narrative irony relates to Emma—Mr Elton and Harriet see merit in her drawing, 'but had there been much less, or had there been ten times more, the delight and admiration of her two companions would have been the same'; or simply 'she wanted exactly the advice they gave'. When she decides 'it was rather too late in the day to set about being simple-minded and ignorant', we pause for ironic reflection. When she becomes engaged to Mr Knightley, she is 'never struck with any sense of injury to her nephew Henry whose rights as heir expectant had formerly been so tenaciously regarded'. Irony can come in the form of generalisation: 'Human nature is so well disposed towards those who are in interesting situations, that a young person, who either marries or dies, is sure of being kindly spoken of', or 'It may be possible to do without dancing entirely. Instances have been known of young people passing many, many months successively, without being at any ball of any description, and no material injury accrue either to body or mind', or simply 'A young lady who faints, must be recovered'.

Literary irony

Part of the irony of *Emma* lies in the fact that real life is not like romantic literature. Emma's fancy leads her to confuse the two: Harriet Smith, because she is beautiful, must be capable of marrying a gentleman; because she is illegitimate her parents must be rich or noble (another cliché of fictional romance). Because Jane Fairfax has been saved from being 'dashed into the sea' by Mr Dixon, Emma jumps to the conclusion (natural for any novel-reader) that she is in love with him. Because Frank Churchill is handsome and writes a handsome letter, she decides before meeting him that they are bound to marry; and because he opens his mouth to say something serious to her for once, she decides that he must be about to propose marriage. This is the stock-in-trade of romance, shown up by being set in 'real life'. The mere comment that 'the wedding was very much like other weddings' cuts across centuries of romantic literature, as does the ironic fact that it is only Mr Woodhouse's fear of poultry-thieves that finally allows Mr Knightley and Emma to marry, to protect the turkeys.

Part 4

Hints for study

Rereading

The first necessity for studying *Emma* is, of course, to read it; the second is to reread it. The great joy of a second reading is that of being able to relish the full irony of certain situations. In every novel, we know on rereading what is 'going to happen', but *Emma* offers something more. We get a new view, for example, of the scenes in which Emma is painting Harriet's portrait, with Mr Elton in close attendance. On a second reading, we realise how dangerously Emma is letting the situation get out of hand; Mr Elton's gallantries and hints ('no married couples at present') are directed at her, not Harriet. We see even more comedy in Emma's pretended broken bootlace as she leaves what she thinks is the doting couple alone. There are more subtle points, too, which emerge on a second reading: we pick up Emma's own thoughts about Mr Elton's silliness and 'parade', and as she thinks them we anticipate the scene in the carriage, savouring its full horror because we know she despises him. As Emma leaps to the conclusion that Frank Churchill is going to propose to her, we know that he is in fact about to tell her about his engagement to Jane Fairfax, so we know the thoughts that both are thinking, as well as their words (which we now see are often quite different).

Our understanding of the characters also gains immeasurably from a second reading. We get a different perspective on Jane Fairfax: her reserve is shown to be the result not of coldness but of an almost intolerable pressure, and we view from a new perspective every scene in which she has to sing in public with Frank Churchill or listen to him singing with Emma. Frank Churchill's character also appears differently to us when we know of the engagement; he becomes less frivolous in our eyes (going to London not to have his hair cut but to order a piano) but also more cruel, callous and materialistic. We see him as cruel when he flirts with or makes hints to Emma in front of Jane Fairfax; we see him as callous in using Emma as a 'blind' so that people will not guess that he is interested in Jane; we see him as materialistic in his refusal to acknowledge his engagement while Mrs Churchill is alive, lest she disapprove and disinherit him. Emma's own character also is seen more fully on a second reading; we comprehend her fallibility at the beginning much more, and realise that she is not helping but destroying Harriet; we understand much earlier that she is in love with Mr Knightley, and can judge her reactions (for example to the idea of his marrying Jane Fairfax) more clearly. We sympathise with her more too because we know that by the end of the novel she has felt shame for her own faults and suffered for them in agonised reflection, which has helped towards a better understanding of herself.

In rereading the novel, think of the following matters: irony, character, Emma's fancy, and 'signs and signals'. The notes below will help you to focus on the relevant passages.

Irony

Notice all passages with Mr Elton, Harriet and Emma (Chapters 4, 5, 6 and 9); John Knightley's warning, and Emma's reaction (Chapter 13); the Westons' party (Chapter 14).

Notice all scenes in which Emma and Frank Churchill discuss Jane Fairfax (Chapters 26, 30 and 41) and Jane Fairfax's non-description of Frank Churchill (Chapter 20).

Character

Consider how the new view of the characters alters your assessment of them: Mr Elton seems less silly and more purposeful when we know he is trying to impress Emma; Frank Churchill less thoughtless and more cruel; Jane Fairfax more strained, long-suffering and likeable, and less chilly and perfectionist. Emma herself seems more stupid and less competent when we know the outcome of her machinations. Mr Knightley appears to us more human and less dictatorial when we know that he chides Emma from love, not superiority; his attitude to Frank Churchill seems less balanced and judicial when we know that he is jealous of him. Harriet rises in our estimation when we realise that she probably loved Robert Martin all the time and was pushed at other people by Emma.

Emma's fancy

On the first reading we may not fully grasp how misleading Emma's fancy is. When we know that Frank Churchill was trying to tell her of his engagement, we see how precipitate it was of her to think he was proposing to her. We see that it is only romantic fantasising that makes her think that Frank Churchill loves Harriet. We understand too that her 'fancy' that she will never marry—and also that Mr Knightley will never marry—are merely the utterances of her as yet unacknowledged heart.

Signs and signals

There are numerous 'clues' to the intrigue of *Emma* which we may not notice in our first reading. Jane Austen weaves them into the novel with great subtlety and skill. See, for example, the passages with Mr Elton and the portrait (Chapter 6) or the charade (Chapter 9), and his interest in Emma's potential sore throat instead of Harriet's actual one. Look for the many signals about Frank Churchill and Jane Fairfax; they have met at Weymouth, 'had sung together once or twice, it appeared, at Weymouth', had danced together at Weymouth. We notice that he does not visit Highbury at all until Jane Fairfax is there; we notice clues too in her embarrassment about walking to the post office, her 'blush of guilt over Colonel Campbell's gift'. We grasp (if we did not do so on first reading) the significance of Frank Churchill's knowing about Mr Perry's new carriage, which only the Bateses and Jane Fairfax had heard about. Frank Churchill's letter (Chapter 50) is an excellent guide to the intricacies of the intrigue, and all the events he mentions in it are detectable from signs and clues within the novel. We are also struck by small points such as his happening to be returning a pair of scissors to the Bateses when he rescues Harriet from the gipsies. There are signs that Emma and Mr Knightley are in love with each other, which we may interpret before they do so themselves: their familiarity ('We always say what we like to one another'; his words 'I love to look at her' (Chapter 5); the quiet way they co-operate to get the visitors home from Randalls in the snow (Chapter 14).

Chapters for intensive study

There are certain key chapters which can be intensively studied with profit. They fall into the categories of 'set piece', of 'event' and of 'reflection'. Look at the way in which Jane Austen leads up to them, how she sets the scene, and what role they play in the progress of the novel.

Set pieces

The 'set pieces' are those large gatherings of people in one place which materially alter the relationships of the characters, things afterwards never being quite the same as before. They are: the Westons' dinner party (Chapters 14–15), the Coles' party (Chapter 26), Emma's party for the Eltons (Chapters 34–6), and the ball at the Crown Inn (Chapter 38). There are also the two memorable outdoor parties: the strawberry picking at Donwell Abbey (Chapter 42), and the picnic at Box Hill (Chapter 43). Notice how much our anticipation is built up for each beforehand: the Coles' party by Emma's indecision about whether or not to go, and her wondering if she is not going to receive an invitation; the Westons' dinner party by doubts about the possibility of persuading Mr Woodhouse to go to it, and Mr John Knightley's forebodings; Emma's dinner party for the Eltons by her distaste for Mrs Elton and her preparations for the guests. The party to Donwell is led up to in excruciating detail by Mrs Elton who wishes to do everything from talking to the housekeeper, to being the 'Lady Patroness', to arriving on a donkey. She also tries to manage the party to Box Hill; from early on we hear about the Sucklings, their arrival and non-arrival, and the lame horse which postpones the outing.

The most masterly build-up of anticipation is for the ball. From the moment Frank Churchill first puts forward the idea (Chapter 24) it is being talked about in Highbury, put off and put on again according to his departures and arrivals, changed from one venue to another, and finally, after a flourish of preparatory detail, dazzling us in Chapter 38.

The way in which the set pieces are described is varied with great skill. The dinner party at the Westons is seen through Emma's eyes, blurred by her annoyance at the attentions of Mr Elton; that at the Coles also through her eyes, rose-tinted by her delight at the attentions of Frank Churchill. Her party for the Eltons is a very detailed study in the movements and conversations of a group of people in formal surroundings. The strawberry picking at Donwell is remarkable for its descriptions of the scenery and atmosphere of an English estate; and the outing to Box Hill for its concentration on the tensions of those taking part. The ball at the Crown is again outstanding, for its vivid description through the mouth of Miss Bates.

The changes of direction in the story made by these set pieces are as follows: the Westons' party throws Emma and Mr Elton together for the declaration; the Coles' party shows her and Frank Churchill openly together; her own dinner party cements her good relations with Mr Knightley; the ball actually finds them dancing together. The day at Donwell suggests harmony with Mr Knightley, the day at Box Hill provides disharmony.

Events

The most powerful 'events' in the novel are all conversations. The first of these is Mr Elton's declaration; others are Emma's quarrel with Mr Knightley over Harriet (Chapter 8), their reconciliation (Chapter 12), and his declaration of love to her (Chapter 49). One could also add Emma's unseemly conversation and rudeness to Miss Bates at Box HIll (Chapter 43) and Mr Elton's public refusal to dance with Harriet at the ball (Chapter 38). These are all high points of the novel, memorable and sharply outlined.

Reflection

The chapters in which Emma reflects on her own blunders, experiences humiliation and resolves to improve, are crucial to the development of the novel, and to our understanding of Emma's own development. They are Chapter 16, in which she feels fury at her own misjudgement of the situation between Harriet and Mr Elton, pity for Harriet, and determination never to meddle again; the end of Chapter 43 and the beginning of Chapter 44, in which she is mortified at Mr Knightley's reproach for her rudeness to Miss Bates; and Chapters 47 and 48, in which she feels shock that Harriet loves Mr Knightley and he apparently loves her, and in which she analyses her own sentiments towards him in depth. These passages of reflection should be studied carefully, watching for the progression from one mood or emotion to another.

Style

Emma is an orderly book. It can be studied in an orderly way, by picking out salient features and subdividing them. The narrative and the dialogue both have balanced and orderly characteristics: look at and distinguish between the passages told by the narrator; the passages spoken by the characters; the passages of conversation related in indirect speech by the narrator; and the passages thought by the characters. You will find examples of all these ways of telling the story in Part 3, Commentary, above. Look first of all at the typically balanced, antithetical and sequential sentences in them, and then note particularly when the orderly pattern changes to an erratic one, broken up by dashes and exclamation marks. You will find examples of smooth and broken style in Part 3, Commentary, and every chapter of *Emma* will afford you further examples.

Characters

In looking at the characters in *Emma*, consider how they are revealed: through the narrator, with succinct summings-up of their major features; through their own words; through other people's conversation. You will find that almost every time we meet a new character, the narrator will sum him up. Description can be direct, as is that of 'Mr Woodhouse: 'having been a valetudinarian all his life, without activity of mind or body, he was a much older man in ways than in years; and though everywhere beloved for the friendliness of his heart and his amiable temper, his talents could not have recommended him at any time'; or it can be through the eyes of Emma, as is the description of Frank Churchill: 'he was a *very* good looking young man; height, air, address, all were unexceptionable, and his countenance had a great deal of the spirit and liveliness of his father's; he looked quiet and sensible'.

Where characters are very talkative, like Miss Bates and Mrs Elton, their characters are easily seen in their own talk. Miss Bates shows herself to be responsive and kind—analyse any of her conversations and you will find it full of thanks, praise of others, and friendliness (see her monologues in Chapters 27, 38 and 44). Mrs Elton betrays her vulgarity and over-familiarity every time she mentions anyone at Highbury, or her acquaintance in London and Bristol. See how comically she betrays her flashiness in describing her simple tastes (Chapters 32–6 and 42).

Society

It is obvious that *Emma* is not simply about 'characters' but about 'characters in society'. You should notice not just the habits and characteristics of each person, but how they affect the people around them. Mr Woodhouse's selfishness is not confined to himself and his family only: it spreads in ripples throughout Highbury. Frank Churchill's decision to keep his engagement secret affects not just Jane Fairfax and himself, but all the other people whom they put in false positions. This relative view of action and character is crucial in Jane Austen's work—see the sections on 'Introverts and Extroverts' and 'Relationships' in Part 3, Commentary. Remember, too, that the way one lived, and the rank one held, mattered deeply to the people that Jane Austen was describing. See the sections on 'Society' and 'Rank and Money' in Part 3, Commentary.

Some sample questions

(1) Discuss the different kinds of irony in *Emma*.
(2) In what ways do the various backgrounds in *Emma* affect the novel?
(3) Discuss the way of life in early nineteenth century England, as seen in *Emma*.
(4) What are the patterns of dramatic tension in *Emma*?
(5) How does a second reading of *Emma* alter our opinions of (a) Frank Churchill; (b) Jane Fairfax; (c) Mr Elton; (d) Emma?
(6) What are Jane Austen's views of the individual's role in society, as seen in *Emma*?
(7) At Box Hill, Frank Churchill announces that Emma wants to know what everyone is thinking. Attempt to supply an answer to this question.
(8) 'Interior action' is more important than 'exterior action' in *Emma*. Do you agree?
(9) Comment on the attitudes of men to women, and vice versa, in *Emma*.

Further questions and model answers

(10) *How is character revealed in* Emma*?*

Jane Austen uses several complementary methods of outlining and filling-in her characters. The narrator usually gives a crisp assessment of each person as he or she is introduced; this is particularly marked in the first chapters in which first the Woodhouses and then their friends are described. People also reveal themselves through their conversations, sometimes consciously, as when Emma refers to her own 'odd humours', but more frequently unconsciously, as when Mrs Elton reveals her vulgarity in her efforts to be refined. Isabella and Emma unconsciously show their best qualities when they placate their father, encouraging him, comforting him and distracting him. There are numerous conversations in which one of the characters is discussed by his or her friends; the most revealing example of this is the discussion of Emma by Mr Knightley and Mrs Weston, in which her good and bad points are aired early enough in the book for us to confirm or contradict them for ourselves through her actions. Mr Knightley often takes part in such conversations: he discusses Harriet, the Eltons, Jane Fairfax, Frank Churchill and others in great detail with Emma, often guiding or warning her, but sometimes laughing at them, in particular Mrs Elton.

In the case of Emma herself, Jane Austen uses a very detailed examination of her thoughts to tell us about her character. This may be done by simply telling us what Emma thought about a certain place (Donwell) or event (the Coles' party). Often the flights of Emma's fancy are traced, so that even if we are aware of what is really happening, we also know in detail what Emma is imagining—for example, when Emma is sure that her plans for bringing Harriet and Mr Elton are succeeding. But the most original method that Jane Austen uses for the revelation of character is by the very elaborate system of self-examination into which Emma is forced every time she is defeated and humiliated. In these passages, not only her present emotions, but her past actions, the motives for them, the misjudgements that prompted them, are held up to the closest scrutiny, providing a minute analysis of her own character.

(11) *The characters in* Emma *can best be polarised into 'active' and 'passive'. Do you agree?*

One can certainly recognise two groups of people in *Emma*: those who are extremely active, and those who are passive. The active women include Emma herself, who is always inaugurating, planning or organising something, whether it is a dinner party or a love affair; Isabella, always occupied in a maternal or wifely way; Mrs Elton, a would-be organiser and initiator of outings and schemes. The active men are Frank Churchill, forever coming and going, planning a ball or a silly game, flirting, sulking, visiting, flattering.

Mr Weston is socially active, Mr Elton is active in his own interests, delighted to read to the painter and sitter, to go out to dinner, to dance. Mr Knightley is a self-contained, sensible, businesslike man who is independent, strong and active. The passive women are Harriet, Jane Fairfax and Miss Bates: Harriet because her suggestible and malleable temperament allows the strong-willed Emma to direct her; Jane Fairfax, who is frozen into inertia by the necessity for circumspection about her engagement with Frank Churchill; Miss Bates because her poverty compels her to accept what people send her, be it apples, loins of pork or invitations. She can never offer, only receive, in purely material terms; verbally, however, she might be classed as 'active'. Of the male characters, only Mr Woodhouse seems totally passive; he has manoeuvred himself into a state in which everything is done for him, and he need make no effort.

The distinction between 'active' and 'passive' is a useful one in examining the people in the novel; but like any other polarity, it is not exclusive. One can also categorise them as 'extrovert' and 'introvert', 'developing' and 'static', 'open' and 'concealed' characters, or as characters who are ruled by their hearts *or* their heads.

---

(12) *Discuss the attitudes to marriage in* Emma.

In the 'happy ending' of *Emma*, three couples are married: Robert Martin and Harriet Smith after a long separation caused by Emma's interference and Harriet's weakness, Frank Churchill and Jane Fairfax after a long separation caused by his materialism; and Mr Knightley and Emma after a long separation caused by their earlier man-to-child relationship and by Emma's lack of understanding of her own heart. The novel is about the events leading up to the marriages; the marriages are seen by all, including the narrator, as a happy and successful outcome. But it is made clar that these marriages are suitable only because of the equality of the man and the woman in each couple. It is made quite clear throughout the novel that where there is inequality of rank, education or ability there cannot be true love. The Westons are agreeably alike; the Eltons ludicrously so. This does not mean that the man and the woman should be equally intelligent: John Knightley and Isabella are opposites in that respect; but she has an instinctive intelligence in humouring him, and in mothering his children, that makes her his complementary opposite.

Great emphasis is laid on the financial and 'class' aspects of marriage. Emma is pleased that Isabella has made an excellent marriage into a rich and secure family with land and 'untainted' blood; she discounts any 'inequalities of temper' in John Knightley, and hardly considers an attraction or compatibility between the two. We should understand and not condemn this materialistic view of marriage; there were fixed conventions which governed the orderly society that Jane Austen lived in and admired, and it was unacceptable within them to marry far above or below one's class. Marriage was not simply love between two people, nor a sacrament of the church: it was a social contract, and should follow the rules of convention and tradition for the greater happiness of the couple themselves and of the society they lived in.

Part 5

Suggestions for further reading

The text

The text of *Emma* used in these notes is that of the Penguin English Library, edited with an introduction by Ronald Blythe, Penguin Books, Harmondsworth, 1966, many times reprinted.

Other novels by Jane Austen

Sense and Sensibility, The Oxford Illustrated Jane Austen, 3rd edition, Oxford University Press, London, 1965.

Pride and Prejudice, The Oxford Illustrated Jane Austen, revised edition, Oxford University Press, London, 1965.

Mansfield Park, The Oxford Illustrated Jane Austen, revised edition, Oxford University Press, London, 1966.

Northanger Abbey and *Persuasion,* The Oxford Illustrated Jane Austen, revised edition, Oxford University Press, London, 1969.

These are all edited by R. W. Chapman, with excellent introductions and notes. These novels also appear in the Oxford English Novels series, and in the Penguin English Library.

Juvenile and unfinished works

Juvenilia, Early Work, and *Fragments; Lady Susan; The Watsons; Sanditon* are all reprinted in *Minor Works,* the Oxford Illustrated Jane Austen, Vol. VI, Oxford University Press, London, 1954.

Lady Susan; The Watsons; Sanditon are republished in the Penguin English Library, Penguin Books, Harmondsworth, 1966.

Jane Austen's Letters, ed. R. W. Chapman, Oxford University Press, London, revised edition, 1959.

The life of Jane Austen

AUSTEN-LEIGH, JAMES: *A Memor of Jane Austen*, 2nd edition, Bentley, London, 1871. The first biography of Jane Austen, written by her nephew. It contains interesting family details.

LASKI, MARGHANITA: *Jane Austen and Her World,* Thames and Hudson, London, 1969. Excellent pictures of Jane Austen and the life of her day.

Criticism of Jane Austen

CRAIK, W. A.: *Jane Austen in Her Time,* Methuen, London, 1969. Good on the novels and their context.

CRAIK, W. A.: *Jane Austen, The Six Novels,* University Paperbacks Series, Methuen, London, 1965. Excellent on characterisation and style.

DUCKWORTH, ALISTAIR M.: *The Improvement of the Estate,* Johns Hopkins Press, Baltimore and London, 1971. A good account of the culture and morality of Jane Austen's times.

LITZ, A. WALTON: *Jane Austen: a Study of Her Artistic Development*, Oxford University Press, London and New York, 1965. A comprehensive account of the literary and moral background to Jane Austen's work.

LODGE, DAVID (ED.): *Emma, A Casebook,* Macmillan, London, 1968. A very full collection of criticism of *Emma* from the first reviews of the book up to the 1960s.

MUDRICK, MARVIN: *Jane Austen: Irony as Defense and Discovery*, Princeton University Press, Princeton, 1952. A controversial account of Jane Austen's irony.

PAGE, NORMAN: *The Language of Jane Austen,* Blackwell, Oxford, 1962. Jane Austen's technique analysed.

PINION, F. B.: *A Jane Austen Companion;* Macmillan, London, 1973. A splendid handbook to Jane Austen's life and work and to the social conventions of the time, with a glossary of outdated words and a good bibliography.

WRIGHT, ANDREW H.: *Jane Austen's Novels: a Study in Structure*, Pelican Books, Harmondsworth, 1972. A handy guide to the novels and to Jane Austen's themes and materials.

The author of these notes

BARBARA HAYLEY is a Senior Lecturer in English at St Patrick's College, Maynooth. She was educated at Trinity College Dublin and the University of Kent at Canterbury. After a business career in London she was a Gulbenkian Research Fellow at the University of Cambridge, and a Fellow of Lucy Cavendish College. Her publications include *A Biblio-graphy of the Writings of William Carleton; Carleton's Traits and Stories and the Nineteenth Century Anglo-Irish Tradition;* and York Notes on Sean O'Casey's *Juno and the Paycock,* Jane Austen's *Mansfield Park* and Gavin Maxwell's *Ring of Bright Water.*

York Notes: list of titles

CHINUA ACHEBE
A Man of the People
Arrow of God
Things Fall Apart

EDWARD ALBEE
Who's Afraid of Virginia Woolf?

ELECHI AMADI
The Concubine

ANONYMOUS
Beowulf
Everyman

JOHN ARDEN
Serjeant Musgrave's Dance

AYI KWEI ARMAH
The Beautyful Ones Are Not Yet Born

W. H. AUDEN
Selected Poems

JANE AUSTEN
Emma
Mansfield Park
Northanger Abbey
Persuasion
Pride and Prejudice
Sense and Sensibility

HONORÉ DE BALZAC
Le Père Goriot

SAMUEL BECKETT
Waiting for Godot

SAUL BELLOW
Henderson, The Rain King

ARNOLD BENNETT
Anna of the Five Towns

WILLIAM BLAKE
Songs of Innocence, Songs of Experience

ROBERT BOLT
A Man For All Seasons

ANNE BRONTË
The Tenant of Wildfell Hall

CHARLOTTE BRONTË
Jane Eyre

EMILY BRONTË
Wuthering Heights

ROBERT BROWNING
Men and Women

JOHN BUCHAN
The Thirty-Nine Steps

JOHN BUNYAN
The Pilgrim's Progress

BYRON
Selected Poems

ALBERT CAMUS
L'Etranger (The Outsider)

GEOFFREY CHAUCER
Prologue to the Canterbury Tales
The Clerk's Tale
The Franklin's Tale
The Knight's Tale
The Merchant's Tale
The Miller's Tale
The Nun's Priest's Tale
The Pardoner's Tale
The Wife of Bath's Tale
Troilus and Criseyde

ANTON CHEKOV
The Cherry Orchard

SAMUEL TAYLOR COLERIDGE
Selected Poems

WILKIE COLLINS
The Moonstone
The Woman in White

SIR ARTHUR CONAN DOYLE
The Hound of the Baskervilles

WILLIAM CONGREVE
The Way of the World

JOSEPH CONRAD
Heart of Darkness
Lord Jim
Nostromo
The Secret Agent
Victory
Youth and *Typhoon*

STEPHEN CRANE
The Red Badge of Courage

BRUCE DAWE
Selected Poems

WALTER DE LA MARE
Selected Poems

DANIEL DEFOE
A Journal of the Plague Year
Moll Flanders
Robinson Crusoe

CHARLES DICKENS
A Tale of Two Cities
Bleak House
David Copperfield
Dombey and Son
Great Expectations
Hard Times
Little Dorrit
Nicholas Nickleby
Oliver Twist
Our Mutual Friend
The Pickwick Papers

EMILY DICKINSON
Selected Poems

JOHN DONNE
Selected Poems

THEODORE DREISER
Sister Carrie

GEORGE ELIOT
Adam Bede
Middlemarch
Silas Marner
The Mill on the Floss

T. S. ELIOT
Four Quartets
Murder in the Cathedral
Selected Poems
The Cocktail Party
The Waste Land

J. G. FARRELL
The Siege of Krishnapur

GEORGE FARQUHAR
The Beaux Stratagem

WILLIAM FAULKNER
Absalom, Absalom!
As I Lay Dying
Go Down, Moses
The Sound and the Fury

HENRY FIELDING
Joseph Andrews
Tom Jones

F. SCOTT FITZGERALD
Tender is the Night
The Great Gatsby

E. M. FORSTER
A Passage to India
Howards End

ATHOL FUGARD
Selected Plays

JOHN GALSWORTHY
Strife

MRS GASKELL
North and South

WILLIAM GOLDING
Lord of the Flies
The Inheritors
The Spire

OLIVER GOLDSMITH
She Stoops to Conquer
The Vicar of Wakefield

ROBERT GRAVES
Goodbye to All That

GRAHAM GREENE
Brighton Rock
The Heart of the Matter
The Power and the Glory

THOMAS HARDY
Far from the Madding Crowd
Jude the Obscure
Selected Poems
Tess of the D'Urbervilles
The Mayor of Casterbridge
The Return of the Native
The Trumpet Major
The Woodlanders
Under the Greenwood Tree

L. P. HARTLEY
The Go-Between
The Shrimp and the Anemone

NATHANIEL HAWTHORNE
The Scarlet Letter

SEAMUS HEANEY
Selected Poems

JOSEPH HELLER
Catch-22

ERNEST HEMINGWAY
A Farewell to Arms
For Whom the Bell Tolls
The African Stories
The Old Man and the Sea

GEORGE HERBERT
Selected Poems

HERMANN HESSE
Steppenwolf

BARRY HINES
Kes

HOMER
The Iliad
The Odyssey

ANTHONY HOPE
The Prisoner of Zenda

GERARD MANLEY HOPKINS
Selected Poems

WILLIAM DEAN HOWELLS
The Rise of Silas Lapham

RICHARD HUGHES
A High Wind in Jamaica

THOMAS HUGHES
Tom Brown's Schooldays

ALDOUS HUXLEY
Brave New World

HENRIK IBSEN
A Doll's House
Ghosts
Hedda Gabler

HENRY JAMES
Daisy Miller
The Ambassadors
The Europeans
The Portrait of a Lady
The Turn of the Screw
Washington Square

SAMUEL JOHNSON
Rasselas

BEN JONSON
The Alchemist
Volpone

JAMES JOYCE
A Portrait of the Artist as a Young Man
Dubliners

JOHN KEATS
Selected Poems

RUDYARD KIPLING
Kim

D. H. LAWRENCE
Sons and Lovers
The Rainbow
Women in Love

CAMARA LAYE
L'Enfant Noir

HARPER LEE
To Kill a Mocking-Bird

LAURIE LEE
Cider with Rosie

THOMAS MANN
Tonio Kröger

CHRISTOPHER MARLOWE
Doctor Faustus
Edward II

ANDREW MARVELL
Selected Poems

W. SOMERSET MAUGHAM
Of Human Bondage
Selected Short Stories

GAVIN MAXWELL
Ring of Bright Water

J. MEADE FALKNER
Moonfleet

HERMAN MELVILLE
Billy Budd
Moby Dick

THOMAS MIDDLETON
Women Beware Women

THOMAS MIDDLETON *and* WILLIAM ROWLEY
The Changeling

ARTHUR MILLER
Death of a Salesman
The Crucible

JOHN MILTON
Paradise Lost I & II
Paradise Lost IV & IX
Selected Poems

V. S. NAIPAUL
A House for Mr Biswas

SEAN O'CASEY
Juno and the Paycock
The Shadow of a Gunman

GABRIEL OKARA
The Voice

EUGENE O'NEILL
Mourning Becomes Electra

GEORGE ORWELL
Animal Farm
Nineteen Eighty-four

JOHN OSBORNE
Look Back in Anger

WILFRED OWEN
Selected Poems

ALAN PATON
Cry, The Beloved Country

THOMAS LOVE PEACOCK
Nightmare Abbey and *Crotchet Castle*

HAROLD PINTER
The Birthday Party
The Caretaker

PLATO
The Republic

ALEXANDER POPE
Selected Poems

THOMAS PYNCHON
The Crying of Lot 49

SIR WALTER SCOTT
Ivanhoe
Quentin Durward
The Heart of Midlothian
Waverley

PETER SHAFFER
The Royal Hunt of the Sun

WILLIAM SHAKESPEARE
A Midsummer Night's Dream
Antony and Cleopatra
As You Like It
Coriolanus
Cymbeline
Hamlet
Henry IV Part I
Henry IV Part II
Henry V
Julius Caesar
King Lear
Love's Labour Lost
Macbeth
Measure for Measure
Much Ado About Nothing
Othello
Richard II
Richard III
Romeo and Juliet
Sonnets
The Merchant of Venice
The Taming of the Shrew
The Tempest
The Winter's Tale
Troilus and Cressida
Twelfth Night
The Two Gentlemen of Verona

GEORGE BERNARD SHAW
Androcles and the Lion
Arms and the Man
Caesar and Cleopatra
Candida
Major Barbara
Pygmalion
Saint Joan
The Devil's Disciple

MARY SHELLEY
Frankenstein

PERCY BYSSHE SHELLEY
Selected Poems

RICHARD BRINSLEY SHERIDAN
The School for Scandal
The Rivals

WOLE SOYINKA
The Lion and the Jewel
The Road
Three Shorts Plays

EDMUND SPENSER
The Faerie Queene (Book I)

JOHN STEINBECK
Of Mice and Men
The Grapes of Wrath
The Pearl

LAURENCE STERNE
A Sentimental Journey
Tristram Shandy

ROBERT LOUIS STEVENSON
Kidnapped
Treasure Island
Dr Jekyll and Mr Hyde

TOM STOPPARD
Professional Foul
Rosencrantz and Guildenstern are Dead

JONATHAN SWIFT
Gulliver's Travels

JOHN MILLINGTON SYNGE
The Playboy of the Western World

TENNYSON
Selected Poems

W. M. THACKERAY
Vanity Fair

DYLAN THOMAS
Under Milk Wood

EDWARD THOMAS
Selected Poems

FLORA THOMPSON
Lark Rise to Candleford

J. R. R. TOLKIEN
The Hobbit
The Lord of the Rings

CYRIL TOURNEUR
The Revenger's Tragedy

ANTHONY TROLLOPE
Barchester Towers

MARK TWAIN
Huckleberry Finn
Tom Sawyer

JOHN VANBRUGH
The Relapse

VIRGIL
The Aeneid

VOLTAIRE
Candide

EVELYN WAUGH
Decline and Fall
A Handful of Dust

JOHN WEBSTER
The Duchess of Malfi
The White Devil

H. G. WELLS
The History of Mr Polly
The Invisible Man
The War of the Worlds

ARNOLD WESKER
Chips with Everything
Roots

PATRICK WHITE
Voss

OSCAR WILDE
The Importance of Being Earnest

TENNESSEE WILLIAMS
The Glass Menagerie

VIRGINIA WOOLF
Mrs Dalloway
To the Lighthouse

WILLIAM WORDSWORTH
Selected Poems

WILLIAM WYCHERLEY
The Country Wife

W. B. YEATS
Selected Poems